Chasing a Grand Illusion:
Replacing Deterrence With Disarmament

Keith B. Payne

Foreword By Brad Roberts

National Institute Press®

Published by
National Institute Press®
9302 Lee Highway, Suite 750
Fairfax, Virginia 22031

Library of Congress Control Number: 2023932838

Publisher's Cataloging-in-Publication
(Provided by Cassidy Cataloguing Services, Inc.)
Names: Payne, Keith B., author.
Title: Chasing a grand illusion : replacing deterrence with disarmament / Keith B. Payne.
Description: Fairfax, Virginia : National Institute Press, [2023] | Includes bibliographical references and index.
Identifiers: ISBN: 979-8-218-14756-3 | LCCN: 2023932838
Subjects: LCSH: Deterrence (Strategy)--Moral and ethical aspects. | Deterrence (Strategy)--Religious aspects. | Nuclear weapons--Moral and ethical aspects. | Nuclear weapons--Religious aspects. | Just war doctrine. | Nuclear disarmament. | Unilateral disarmament. | National security. | Military policy. | Non-provocative defense (Military science)
Classification: LCC: JZ5625 .P39 2023 | DDC: 327.1/74--dc23

This text draws from the author's previous works: *Tilting at Windmills: Nuclear Disarmament Advocacy in an Anarchic World Order, Information Series*, No. 540, November 22, 2022; *Shadows on the Wall: Deterrence and Disarmament*, 2020; and (with Dr. Karl Payne) *A Just Defense*, 1987.

Cover design by Stephanie Koeshall.

For Claire, Sarabeth, David and Nathaniel,
with hope and optimism.

And in memory of John Holland Payne.

Acknowledgments

I would like to express my enormous gratitude for the professors and professional mentors who devoted work, time and attention to my academic and professional development, and thereby made this text possible. There are many who did so, but most notably are Professor Kenneth N. Waltz and Professor Ernst B. Haas at U.C. Berkeley, Professor William R. Van Cleave at the University of Southern California, Dr. Colin S. Gray, Dr. Herman Kahn, Dr. James Schlesinger and Dr. John S. Foster Jr. Absent any plan on my part, I benefited greatly from each of these gentlemen.

I also would like to thank Dr. Brad Roberts for his thoughtful *Foreword* for this text and the senior national security practitioners and academics who provided their review comments on it, included on pages 91-99.

Once again, I owe great thanks to Amy Joseph of National Institute who worked so patiently and diligently through numerous drafts and revisions to help turn the manuscript into a publishable text. And, much appreciation to the Sarah Scaife Foundation for providing the resources that made this work possible.

Finally, once again, I am enormously grateful to my wife, Beth, for editing the manuscript so nicely, not once, but twice, and for putting up with my perpetual writing and reading when, undoubtedly, there were other things that needed to be done.

Table of Contents

Foreword

A decade after the failure to abolish nuclear weapons in the immediate aftermath of World War II, Robert Oppenheimer took stock of lessons learned and future prospects. Among those lessons were the following:

- "Disarmament should not be confused with the solution to the problem of nuclear war, and not even very much to the problem of sudden nuclear war."

- "Disarmament is desirable, but only in connection with vast changes in the world, some of which have to do with the international cooperative development, others...with the maintenance of international order, and some...with the establishment of some minimal elements of transnational power."[*]

Nearly seven decades later, these lessons have lost their currency in the debate about nuclear disarmament. The Treaty on the Prohibition of Nuclear Weapons—the nuclear ban treaty—enjoys wide and growing support despite glaring gaps when it comes to the mechanisms necessary to ensure nuclear peace in a disarmed world. And ban treaty advocates, arguing that there has been too much realism in international nuclear diplomacy, have succeeded in turning international diplomacy away from the step-by-step disarmament process envisioned by parties to the Nuclear

---

[*] Given in 1957, the two talks were to a meeting of the American Assembly and to a conference on NATO at Princeton University. The latter was published as Robert Oppenheimer, "The Environs of Atomic Power," in Philip C. Jessup, ed., *Atoms for Power: United States Policy in Atomic Energy Development* (New York, The American Assembly, Columbia University, 1957). See also J. Robert Oppenheimer, "In Keeping of Reason," *Bulletin of Atomic Scientists*, 16 (January 1960). Relevant citations are collected and discussed in Michael A. Day, *The Hope and Vision of J. Robert Oppenheimer* (Singapore: World Scientific, 2016), pp. 32-34.

Non-Proliferation Treaty and toward a process aimed at naming and shaming those who see value in deterrence. In response, many government officials have been reluctant to engage with these arguments, recognizing the age-old truth that disarmament is popular, and deterrence is not. This combination of factors weakens deterrence at a time when it is facing new challenges from revisionist leaders in Moscow and Beijing — leaders aggressively expanding and diversifying their nuclear toolkits.

In this timely and engaging new study, Professor Keith Payne takes up the challenge of restoring some realism to the debate about disarmament. In clear and cogent analysis, he explores the gaps between the rhetoric of disarmers and the reality of disarmament. Working systematically through the disarmament canon, he juxtaposes claims about how the international system should work, or would need to work, with evidence about how it actually works. The result is a useful corrective to many of the beliefs and perceptions that inform disarmament advocacy. At a moment in international affairs when order is eroding and the winds of war are blowing across Europe, clarity about the lessons of the past is more valuable than ever.

The lines of argument presented here should become familiar to anyone interested in the roles of nuclear weapons in the 21st century. Experts in government, think tanks, and academia — including students — will find much to ponder.

Dr. Brad Roberts
Director, Center for Global Security Research
Lawrence Livermore National Laboratory

Preface

In 1910, Sir Norman Angell first published a book entitled, *The Great Illusion: A Study of the Relation of Military Power to National Advantage.* This book went through many editions and was a sensation in much of Europe — being particularly influential in the thinking of the British educated, governing elite at the time. Angell was both knighted and awarded the 1933 Nobel Peace Prize for his powerful work.

Sir Norman's writing was elaborate and nuanced. But the basic thesis of his work was that, given the economic advancement and interdependence of European nations, territorial control and military power no longer were the basis for economic advantage and national prosperity. Continuing to think otherwise was "the Great Illusion." Indeed, Angell emphasized and elaborated the point that wars waged for the purpose of territorial control and associated economic advantages were now more likely to impoverish both winners and losers because war destroys the financial, economic and trade ties that create national wealth in an economically interdependent international system. War, he said, had become irrational because mutual cooperative relations provide the potential for mutual prosperity; war destroys wealth for all; correspondingly, cooperation, not war, is the only rational choice.

Much of this basic thesis was not new. It can be traced back to the considerably earlier narrative that market-based societies prefer peaceful relations and times because cooperative international political relations are the necessary basis for mutually advantageous business and economic relations. But Sir Norman's influential book presented this argument comprehensively. With numerous illustrations and detailed evidence, he drew logical implications that many were eager to hear, i.e., war and military preparations were of sharply declining actual value in the modern world.

In short, Angell speculated that "the need for defence arises from the existence of a motive for attack."[1] His work, however, indicated that the old wealth-based motives for attack no longer held. As leaders increasingly came to the understanding that warlike behaviors and preparations could not provide real benefit, *sensible* citizens and leaders seeking personal and national prosperity increasingly would retreat from supporting warlike behaviors and preparations. The motives for attack would abate, and the corresponding need for armaments to defend against attack would similarly decline.

The engine for this change was simply rational national decision making, based on recognition of the basic facts of economic interdependence and the application of these facts to national behaviors. This would increasingly mandate the striving for peaceful international relations, and the rejection of war and the need to prepare for war. In response to critics, including Admiral Alfred Thayer Mahan, who doubted Angell's expectations or said that such developments were reserved for the distant future, Angell wrote that the "Law of Acceleration" could rapidly drive more amicable and peaceful international relations, and, correspondingly, prudent disarmament moves.[2]

Sir Norman did *not*, in *The Great Illusion*, assure readers that this new reality dictated that there would be no further war. He did argue, however, that as broad communities within European states learned to appreciate the actual advantages of cooperation and the disadvantages of war for winner and loser alike, those communities would rationally seek cooperative transnational ties and move away from

---

[1] Norman Angell, *The Great Illusion: A Study of the Relation of Military Power to National Advantage* (London: William Heinemann, 1912), p. 337.

[2] Ibid., pp. 119, 220.

warlike patterns of behavior. Consequently, Angell suggested strongly that a general European war was becoming increasingly improbable, and elsewhere claimed that, "The cessation of military conflict between powers like France and Germany, or Germany and England, or Russia and Germany...has come already. ... armed Europe is at present engaged in spending most of its time and energy rehearsing a performance which all concerned know is never likely to come off."[3] To help secure this peace, Sir Norman emphasized the need for the rule of international law and an international court to adjudicate conflicts peacefully.

World Wars I and II seemed to both confirm and refute Angell's work: Most winners and losers suffered enormous economic loss but, in contrast to Angell's expectations, the prospect thereof had not moderated the path to war. Had London taken Angell's writing to heart as the basis for its security policies, Britain would likely have been in an even worse position to confront Adolf Hitler in 1939.

Following World War II, after seeing the rise of aggressive, totalitarian rulers in Europe, Sir Norman reportedly lost confidence in his earlier expectations of the coming rule of reason and "law of acceleration," and moved from pacifist peace activist to an ardent supporter of the Atlantic Alliance.[4]

This bit of intellectual history is important to the discussion of this text, which is a follow-on to my 2020 book, *Shadows on the Wall: Deterrence and Disarmament.* Sir Norman presented a thesis that suggested a coming transition in the behavior of the international system toward a new order in which peaceful relations, the rule of

---

[3] Michael Rühle, "The End of the 'Great Illusion': Norman Angell and the Founding of NATO," *NATO Review*, January 14, 2019, available at https://www.nato.int/docu/review/articles/2019/01/14/the-end-of-the-great-illusion-norman-angell-and-the-founding-of-nato/index.html.

[4] As discussed in, Ibid.

law, and disarmament could prevail. He went to great lengths to explain the dynamic, new to international relations, that would drive this revolution in thinking and national behavior. This was, as described, peoples and leaders increasing recognition of the realities of economic interdependence and their rational response to those realities in the form of growing opposition to war and the armaments necessary for war.

The caveat, which Angell fully recognized, was that his revolution in international relations depended on national leaderships moving together to behave in ways that Angell deemed rational, i.e., cooperative vice conflictual. The ultimate dynamic for the revolution outlined in his work was the hope/expectation that national decision making regarding war and armaments would become increasingly rational, according to his expectation of what that implied for nations' behaviors. This, the actual history of the Twentieth Century demonstrated convincingly, was not to be the case.

The subjects of the pages in this text are Cold War and more recent proposals for global nuclear disarmament, both church-based and secular. Those proposals, for all their variety, are in many ways similar to Sir Norman's thesis of 1910. For example, they virtually always describe a transformation of international relations as the necessary basis for disarmament. While the dynamics for this change identified by nuclear disarmament advocates typically are arcane, ambiguous, and/or transcendental, they generally are presented as the basis for expecting greater amity and cooperation among nations, driven by leadership decision making that responds *rationally* to new developments and is codified by some form of global governance. Similar to Sir Norman's thesis, modern nuclear disarmament proposals attribute great power and effect to these dynamics driving the transformation of international relations and leading to nuclear disarmament.

In addition, just as *The Great Illusion* argued strongly *against* the armaments of the day as likely being unnecessary for defense and contrary to the transition Angell projected, contemporary disarmament advocates are extremely critical of nuclear deterrence policies and capabilities — the maintenance of which they contend works against their recommended pursuit of nuclear disarmament as the far safer and more effective alternative to policies of nuclear deterrence. Consequently, proponents of nuclear disarmament often seek to "stigmatize" nuclear weapons and nuclear weapon states.

Whether contemporary church-based and secular proposals for nuclear disarmament — typically predicated on the common premise of a global transition that is driven by unprecedented dynamics shaping national decision making and thus international relations — are plausible is the question explored in this text. If so, they may deserve greater acceptance and consideration as the basis for policy decisions. If not, they should be treated with appropriate skepticism because, as the basis for policy decisions, they could easily undermine Western security. For reasons discussed at length in the following pages, the answer to that question suggests that skepticism rather than acceptance is prudent.

A century after the publication of *The Great Illusion: A Study of the Relation of Military Power to National Advantage,* Sir Norman's "Great Illusion" appears to have been replaced by a wholly different illusion. That new "grand illusion" is the contemporary proposition offered by church-based and secular advocates that nuclear disarmament can replace the need for nuclear deterrence. As emphasized in this text, my conclusion that this proposition is an illusion does not reflect any lack of appreciation for the vision of a cooperative world order and nuclear disarmament. It does, however, reflect deep skepticism regarding its plausibility as envisaged, and thus comparable skepticism about the prudence of U.S. policies that would prioritize that vision over sustaining deterrence.

Why "deep skepticism"? Because, for national leaders reliant on nuclear deterrence for security to forego nuclear capabilities, they likely must first trust that their foes would do the same reliably. Yet, given historical experience, the prospect is very real that one or more nations would cheat on a nuclear disarmament agreement. All compliant nations would then be vulnerable to their less scrupulous foes. Consequently, a powerful global authority capable of monitoring and enforcing agreements is likely necessary for disarmament to be deemed a prudent choice. Yet, the establishment of such a global authority has consistently proven impossible given the enduring, sharp conflicts of interests among nations.

In addition, yielding sovereignty and power to the hypothetical global authority would demand that national leaders also first trust that the global authority itself would reliably act in a conscientious and pristine manner. Yet, unless all prospective leaders and agents of that global authority were to shed seemingly enduring patterns of inconsistent and unscrupulous human behavior, it could immediately pose its own potential threat to its members. Rebellion and a return to conflict would be likely.

Barring the fundamental transformation of humankind, and thus international relations, there appears to be little or no basis for trusting foes or a prospective global authority as necessary for disarmament. That trust seems absent in the past and shows no sign of emerging. It is in light of this harsh reality that leaderships now reliant on nuclear deterrence would have to judge various church-based and secular proposals for disarmament to be prudent. It seems unlikely that many ever would do so.

Dr. Keith B. Payne
Fairfax, Virginia

Introduction

Immediately following the peaceful end of the Cold War, many leaders, academics and commentators were convinced that a "new world order" was emerging — one in which nuclear weapons would play little, if any, role and great power wars would be a thing of the past. Yet, after seemingly disappearing from public consciousness following the end of the Cold War, nuclear weapons and deterrence once again are in the daily spotlight given Moscow's recent excessive use of nuclear threats in its war against Ukraine. A common theme in the commentary offered by many church-based and secular nuclear disarmament advocates is that a policy of nuclear deterrence, such as that of the United States, is unacceptably dangerous and a misguided justification for retaining nuclear weapons — the existence of which poses a perpetual lethal threat to all humankind. The solution to national insecurity concerns is *not* continuing dangerous policies of deterrence, but greater global cooperation and nuclear disarmament. This theme continues to dominate activism on behalf of the United Nation's contemporary nuclear ban treaty:[5] for global safety and security, policies of deterrence must be rejected in favor of nuclear disarmament.

In the early-to-late 1980s, multiple Christian church bodies, denominations, and scholars of religion issued reports and notable books regarding the morality of nuclear arms and deterrence. For example, church-based reports were provided by, *inter alia*, the U.S. Conference of Catholic Bishops and their French and German counterparts, the National Association of Evangelicals, United Methodists, Presbyterian, United Church of Christ, Reformed Church of

---

[5] See for example, Beatrice Fihn and Setsuko Thurlow, "International Campaign to Abolish Nuclear Weapons (ICAN) — Nobel Lecture (English)," *NobelPrize.org*, December 10, 2017, available at https://www.nobelprize.org/prizes/peace/2017/ican/lecture/.

America, and American Lutherans. [6]   While not all of this work is of comparable quality, some is extremely thoughtful and detailed. This level and intensity of church-based scrutiny and commentary regarding the morality of nuclear policies and weapons in general was far less apparent before and after the early-to-late 1980s. Perhaps this is because within a few years of that decade, by the early 1990s, the question appeared passé with the collapse of the Soviet Union and the end of the Cold War—in the West, as noted, nuclear weapons and threats were widely expected to be of rapidly declining significance in international relations.

However, the series of explicit Russian nuclear threats in its contemporary war on Ukraine has brought the subject back to prominence and surveys now suggest that the American public once again fears nuclear war.[7] In addition, the current international effort to ban nuclear weapons by treaty—the Treaty on the Prohibition of Nuclear Weapons—and the considerable media attention given to that effort has compelled governments to choose between adopting, or not, a strict public position for nuclear

---

[6] See a helpful discussion of several of these reports in, Donald Davidson, *Nuclear Weapons and the American Churches* (Boulder, CO: Westview Press, 1983). More recently, see, Drew Christiansen, "Introduction," in, *A World Free from Nuclear Weapons: The Vatican Conference on Disarmament*, edited by Drew Christiansen and Carole Sargent (Washington, D.C.: Georgetown University Press, 2020), pp. xiii-xxiii; and, the Pastoral Letter by Most Reverend John C. Wester, Archbishop of Santa Fe, *Living in the Light of Christ's Peace: A Conversation Toward Nuclear Disarmament* (Albuquerque, NM: Archdiocese of Santa Fe, January 11, 2022).

[7] See for example, Greg Hadley, "American Public's Concern About Nuclear War Growing, Survey Finds," *Air & Space Forces Magazine Online*, December 2, 2022, available at https://www.airandspaceforces.com/american-publics-concern-about-nuclear-war-growing-survey-finds/.

disarmament.[8]   Consequently, the moral and ethical question surrounding nuclear weapons and policy appear, once again, to be emerging as a topic of widespread discussion and analysis.[9]

This text includes a focus on the positions expressed by various scholars of religion and in church-based studies regarding questions of the morality of nuclear weapons and deterrence.   Of particular interest is their frequent promotion of the conclusion that the solution to the threat posed by the existence of nuclear weapons is global nuclear disarmament and *not* what they describe as unacceptably dangerous policies of nuclear deterrence.

Seminal Work and Conclusions

Many of the church-based reports during the period of close attention and interest, although not all, rejected the employment of nuclear weapons, their possession, and any policy of nuclear deterrence or, somewhat more narrowly, rejected their employment while conditionally accepting their possession for deterrence purposes. The U.S. Conference of Catholic Bishops, for example, issued a lengthy report on the subject in 1983, *The Challenge of Peace: God's Promise and Our Response.*[10] It included no categorical condemnation of *all* possible forms of nuclear employment, but definitively rejected most employment options and

---

[8] United Nations, *Treaty on the Prohibition of Nuclear Weapons* (English), available at https://www.un.org>disarmament>wmd>tpnw.

[9] See for example, Brad Roberts, "Nuclear Ethics and the Ban Treaty," in, Bard Nikolas, Vik Steen and Olav Njolstad, *Nuclear Disarmament: A Critical Assessment* (New York: Routledge, 2018), pp. 112-130, available at https://cgsr.llnl.gov/content/assets/docs/Nuclear-Disarmament-A-Critical-Assessment.pdf.

[10] See the American Catholic Bishops' Pastoral Letter in, "The Challenge of Peace: God's Promise and Our Response," *Origins*, Vol. 13, No. 1 (May 19, 1983), pp. 1-32.

repeatedly expressed a strong presumption against *any* possible employment.[11]   Nevertheless, the American Catholic Bishops conditionally accepted the morality of possessing nuclear weapons for deterrence purposes as an interim measure pending nuclear disarmament.[12]

More recently, however, Pope Francis has declared both the possession and employment of nuclear weapons to be "immoral," and that a policy of deterrence is not an acceptable justification for nuclear weapons.[13]   Indeed, Vatican Foreign Minister Dominique Mamberti has observed that the "chief obstacle" to nuclear disarmament

---

[11] For example, "Our no to nuclear war must in the end be definitive and decisive...there must be no misunderstanding of our profound skepticism about the moral acceptability of any use of nuclear weapons. It is obvious that the use of any weapons which violate the principle of discrimination merits unequivocal condemnation." "The Challenge of Peace: God's Promise and Our Response," op. cit., pp. 14, 19; see also pp. 13, 15, 20-21. As William O'Brien, a highly regarded scholar on the subject said, "The Bishops appear to say that there is no morally permissible use of nuclear weapons." William V. O'Brien, "The Bishops' Unfinished Business," *Comparative Strategy*, Vol. 5, No. 2 (1985), p. 114.

[12] See "The Challenge of Peace: God's Promise and Our Response," op. cit., pp. 17-18.

[13] See for example, "Pope's Demand for Nuclear Disarmament," *Japan Times Online*, November 26, 2019, available at https://www.japantimes.co.jp/opinion/2019/11/26/editorials/popes-demand-nuclear-disarmament/#.Xd1zkuhKi70. See also, Philip Pullella, "Pope, in Change From Predecessors, Condemns Nuclear Arsenals for Deterrence," *Reuters*, November 10, 2017, available at https://www.reuters.com/articles/us-vatican-nuclear/pope-in-change-from-predecessors-condemns-nuclear-arsenal-for-deterrence-idUSKBN1DA161. For a concise history of the Vatican's evolving positions regarding nuclear weapons and deterrence see, Christiansen, "Introduction," in, *A World Free from Nuclear Weapons: The Vatican Conference on Disarmament*, op. cit., p. xiii; and, Aaron Bateman, "The Vatican's Nuclear Diplomacy From the Cold War to the Present," *WarOnTheRocks.com*, December 6, 2019, available at https://warontherocks.com/2019/12/the-vaticans-nuclear-diplomacy-from-the-cold-war-to-the-present/.

"is continued adherence to the doctrine of nuclear deterrence."[14] Because a credible policy of nuclear deterrence depends on the possession of nuclear weapons and a sufficiently believable threat to employ them under some circumstances, it is unsurprising that the church-based reports and positions that generally reject the employment *and* possession of nuclear weapons as immoral also reject nuclear deterrence as immoral and identify nuclear disarmament as the alternative.

In contrast, some prominent church-based reports and scholars of religion conclude that moral considerations can *allow* conditional acceptance of a policy of nuclear deterrence, the possession of nuclear weapons, and the potential acceptability of their restricted employment under specific, limited conditions.[15] Even these analyses, however, frequently point to global nuclear disarmament as the *needed and preferred* solution to the threat posed by nuclear weapons, and identify nuclear deterrence as an

---

[14] Quoted in, Christiansen, "Introduction," in, *A World Free from Nuclear Weapons: The Vatican Conference on Disarmament*, op. cit., p. xiv.

[15] See for example, William O'Brien, *The Conduct of Just and Limited War* (New York: Praeger, 1983), pp. 339-345; Paul Ramsey, *The Just War* (New York: University Press of America, 1983), pp. 236-245, *inter alia*; James Schall, S.J., "Risk, Dissuasion and Political Prudence: The German and French Bishops' Approach to Peace and War," in, *Out of Justice, Peace: Joint Pastoral Letter of the West German Bishops, Winning the Peace: Joint Pastoral Letter of the French Bishops*, edited by James Schall, S.J. (San Francisco, CA: Ignatius Press, 1984), p. 13; James Turner Johnson, *Can Modern War Be Just?* (New Haven, Conn.: Yale University Press, 1984), Chapter 2; James Child, *Nuclear War: The Moral Dimension* (London: Transaction Books, 1986), pp. 169-173; John Stott, *Involvement: Being a Responsible Christian in a Non-Christian Society* (Old Tappan, NJ: Fleming H. Revell Co., 1985), pp. 117-150; Kenneth Kanzer, "What Shall We Do About the Nuclear Problem?" *Christianity Today*, January 21, 1983, pp. 10-11; and, Keith Payne and Karl Payne, *A Just Defense* (Portland, OR: Multnomah Press, 1987), pp. 37-60.

acceptable policy only as an interim security necessity until global disarmament.[16]

Disarmament, Deterrence and the Just War Doctrine

The conclusions that the possession and employment of nuclear weapons, and that policies of nuclear deterrence are all immoral are directly contrary to the U.S. deterrence policy that has, and has had, overwhelming bipartisan support in the U.S. Congress and has guided all Democratic and Republican presidential administrations for seven decades.   On what basis do those advocating nuclear disarmament reach these conclusions?

Various Christian theologians and church organizations ostensibly apply the millennia-old Christian Just War Doctrine to questions regarding the morality of the possession and employment of nuclear weapon and to the policy of nuclear deterrence. For those that do so and conclude that possession and/or employment are immoral, the basis for reaching those conclusions generally follow from their judgments that any nuclear employment is likely to violate the Just War Doctrine's requirements for "distinction" and "proportionality."[17]

The reasoning behind these conclusions from the application of the Just War Doctrine to nuclear policy, in short, is as follows: The employment of nuclear weapons would likely be so destructive of civil society globally that it would violate the principle of "distinction," i.e., it would

---

[16] For example, Stott, *Involvement: Being a Responsible Christian in a Non-Christian Society*, op. cit., p. 140.

[17] For useful, concise explanations of the history and principles of the Just War Doctrine see, O'Brien, *The Conduct of Just and Limited War*, op. cit., pp. 1-70; Johnson, *Can Modern War Be Just?*, op. cit., pp. 7-8, and Chapter 2; and, Child, *Nuclear War: The Moral Dimension*, op. cit., pp. 5-32.

likely *not* be possible to intentionally distinguish between combatants and non-combatants – unacceptably harming both alike grievously.

In addition, those so applying the Just War Doctrine also judge that the employment of nuclear weapons would likely lead to such indiscriminate civilian destruction that even the *unintended* violation of the principle of distinction would be so severe that the harm done to innocent civilians would be *disproportional* to any possible just military objective – thereby violating the principle of proportionality. This requirement addresses the question: "Is the good that is being pursued or defended commensurate with the unintended losses that may reasonably be expected?"[18] The American Catholic Bishops' report observes that even a nuclear strike intentionally limited to military targets "could well involve such massive civilian casualties that in our judgement such a strike would be deemed morally disproportionate, even though not intentionally indiscriminate."[19]

Finally, given this potential destructiveness of nuclear war, as noted above, some church-based commentaries conclude that threats of nuclear employment for deterrence purposes that could be executed, either willfully or unintentionally, also are unacceptable. That is, some church-based studies conclude that possessing or employing nuclear weapons is immoral, and there is, correspondingly, no acceptable basis for nuclear deterrence. The United Methodist Bishops, for example, categorically rejected the employment and possession of nuclear weapons and a policy of nuclear deterrence. It labeled the latter "idolatry," and concluded that "…deterrence must no

---

[18] Marcia Sichol, The *Making of a Nuclear Peace: The Task of Today's Just War Theories* (Washington, D.C.: Georgetown University Press 1990), p. 15.

[19] "The Challenge of Peace: God's Promise and Our Response," op. cit., p. 18.

longer receive the churches' blessing, even as a temporary warrant for holding on to nuclear weapons."[20]

It should be noted that these conclusions regarding nuclear weapons and deterrence, based on the Just War Doctrine's requirements for distinction and proportionality, generally are predicated on the expectation that an initial employment of nuclear weapons, however limited, would escalate to the point of indiscriminate and disproportional civil destruction. The American Catholic Bishops' Pastoral Letter, for example, says that while escalation to indiscriminate and disproportional destruction may not be certain, the "burden of proof" is on those who suggest that any use of nuclear weapons would remain limited so that the resultant destruction would adequately distinguish between combatants and non-combatants,[21] i.e., discriminate, and the level of unintended civil destruction would be acceptable given the necessity of employment to achieve the just results, namely, proportional. Many well-informed authorities on the subject have concluded that, in the event of a nuclear war, it is much more likely to be limited than not.[22] However, "proof" that escalation to indiscriminate and disproportional civil destruction would *not* occur is impossible — the future simply is not so

---

[20] United Methodist Church, Council of Bishops, *In Defense of Creation: The Nuclear Crisis and a Just Peace* (United Methodist Publishing House, 1986), pp. 5 (Overview), 34-35 (Foundation Document).

[21] "The Challenge of Peace: God's Promise and Our Response," op. cit., p. 18.

[22] See for example, the testimony of Defense Secretary James Schlesinger in, United States Senate, Committee on Foreign Affairs, Subcommittee on Arms Control, International Law and Organization, *Briefing on Counterforce Attacks*, 93rd Congress, 2nd Session, September 1, 1974, p. 201. See also, Albert Wohstetter, "Bishops, Statesmen and Other Strategists on the Bombing of Innocents," *Commentary*, June 1983, available at https://www.commentary.org/articles/albert-wohlstetter/bishops-statesmen-and-other-strategists-on-the-bombing-of-innocents/.

predictable. Consequently, the assigned burden of proof regarding the necessity for such limitation cannot be met.

While these church-based reports base their rejection of nuclear employment, possession, and deterrence policies on the Just War Doctrine's guidelines against indiscriminate and disproportional civil destruction, they also tend to reject the deployment of both defensive systems and low-yield, highly-accurate nuclear capabilities that could provide a measure of defensive protection for society and more discriminant, proportional nuclear targeting. Their reasoning for opposing defensive and discriminant capabilities that would otherwise seem to comport well with the Just War Doctrine's distinction and proportionality guidelines typically is based on a branch of deterrence theory that suggests that such capabilities would undermine deterrence *stability*.[23] Consequently, many of the church-based assessments are based *not* on the unalloyed application of Just War Doctrine guidelines, but on an amalgam of those guidelines and a particular deterrence theory narrative regarding "stability."

The secular disarmament community's arguments for nuclear disarmament and against deterrence policies generally parallel this Just War Doctrine-based rejection of nuclear weapons and deterrence — albeit typically without direct reference to the Just War Doctrine. This is not entirely surprising. Just War Doctrine guidelines have largely been incorporated into the general Western understanding of moral behavior regarding war, and, correspondingly, are

---

[23] See the discussion in, Keith Payne and Jill Coleman, "Christian Nuclear Pacifism and Just War Theory: Are They Compatible?" *Comparative Strategy*, Vol. 7, No. 1 (Winter 1988), pp. 75-89. See also, Report of the Committee of Inquiry on the Nuclear Issue, Committee on Peace, Episcopal Diocese of Washington, *The Nuclear Dilemma: A Christian Search for Understanding* (Washington, D.C.: Episcopal Diocese of Washington, 1986), p. 66; and, National Conference of Catholic Bishops, *Building Peace: A Report* (Washington, D.C.: United States Catholic Conference, June 1988), pp. 67-72.

the basis for the legal principles recognized and practiced by the United States. For example, Section 1.6.4 of the Department of Defense *Law of War Manual* states that, "The Just War Tradition provides part of the philosophical foundation for the modern law of war and has considered both *jus ad bellum* and *jus in bello*.... The Just War Tradition remains relevant for decisions to employ U.S. military forces and in warfighting."[24] Section 6.18 essentially repeats the Just War Doctrine's distinction and proportionality requirements: "The law of war governs the use of nuclear weapons, just as it governs the use of conventional weapons. For example, nuclear weapons must be directed against military objectives. In addition, attacks using nuclear weapons must not be conducted when the expected incidental harm to civilians is excessive compared to the military advantage expected to be gained."

Secular advocacy for nuclear disarmament, past and present, often begins with graphic descriptions of a "dark nuclear landscape" that is increasingly dangerous,[25] and the horrors of nuclear war to capture attention and support.[26]

---

[24] Department of Defense, *Law of War Manual* (Washington, D.C.: DoD Office of General Counsel, December 2016), p. 26, available at https://dod.defense.gov/Portals/1/Documents/pubs/DoD%20La w%20of%20War%20Manual%20-%20June%202015%20Updated%20Dec%202016.pdf?ver=2016-12-13-172036-190.

[25] Alexander Kmentt, "The Ban Treaty, Two Years After: A Ray of Hope for Nuclear Disarmament," *Bulletin of the Atomic Scientists*, January 23, 2023, available at https://thebulletin.org/2023/01/the-ban-treaty-two-years-after-a-ray-of-hope-for-nuclear-disarmament/#:~:text=Doomsday%20Clock%20announcement-,The%20ban%20treaty%2C%20two%20years%20after%3A%20A%20ray,of%20hope%20for%20nuclear%20disarmament&text=Two%20years%20ago%2C%20on%20January,dangers%20were%20considered%20very%20high.

[26] See for example, International Campaign to Abolish Nuclear Weapons, *No Place to Hide: Nuclear Weapons and the Collapse of Health Care Systems*, February 2022, available at https://d3n8a8pro7vhmx.cloudfront.net/ican/pages/2544/attachment

From that starting point, it quickly moves to the claim that because nuclear war would be horrific beyond description—indiscriminate and disproportional—nuclear weapons must and can be eliminated if leaders can be pressed to muster the good sense needed to eliminate them.[27] This is a long-standing approach to the policy argument in favor of nuclear disarmament and in opposition to deterrence as the solution to the threat of nuclear destruction.[28] As noted, the general thrust of this argument is that nuclear weapons are so destructive and deterrence so risky that it should be self-evident to all rational leaders that they must accept and indeed advocate for nuclear disarmament as the alternative to deterrence policies.[29] Again, these positions that are expressed outside of the Just War Doctrine are similar to those of many church-based reports. They too are directly contrary to U.S. nuclear deterrence policy that has guided Democratic and Republican presidential administrations for seven decades

---

s/original/1644334250/NoPlacetoHide-ICAN-Report-Feb2022-web.pdf?1644334250.

[27] Fihn and Thurlow, "International Campaign to Abolish Nuclear Weapons (ICAN)—Nobel Lecture (English)," op. cit. See also Beatrice Fihn, "Stigmatize and Prohibit: New UN Talks on Nuclear Weapons Start Today," *Huffington Post*, February 2, 2016, available at http://www.huffingtonpost.com/beatrice-fihn/stigmatize-and-prohibit-n_b_9287144.html.

[28] "We also agree that deterrence is morally and legally unacceptable…nuclear deterrence is rife with uncertainty and extremely dangerous." Richard Falk and David Krieger, *The Path to Zero* (Boulder, CO: Paradigm Publishers, 2012), p. 42.

[29] For example, "The [Treaty on the Prohibition of Nuclear Weapons] challenges the core assumption of nuclear deterrence by highlighting that this theory is fraught with uncertainties and risk. Rather than assuming the 'non-use' of nuclear weapons based on the belief in the stability of nuclear deterrence, the [Treaty] assumes the opposite: the instability of nuclear deterrence ultimately leads to nuclear weapon use." Kmentt, "The Ban Treaty, Two Years After: A Ray of Hope for Nuclear Disarmament," op. cit.

and has had equally overwhelming bipartisan support in the U.S. Congress.

In fact, there is little doubt that even a "limited" nuclear war could be horrific beyond description. But it is a banal tautology to say that the elimination of nuclear arms will end the threat of nuclear war. That claim is comparable to saying that universal wealth will end poverty, and universal home ownership will end homelessness. All are truisms, of course: By definition, in the absence of any nuclear weapons, there could be no immediate nuclear threat, and with universal wealth and homeownership, there would be no poverty or homelessness. That much is painfully self-evident. But arguing that these happy conditions would solve the corresponding problems tells us nothing much useful. Indeed, the assertion of this tautology regarding nuclear weapons, however fashionable, identifies no solution to the problem; it simply leaves unanswered the corresponding fundamental underlying questions of whether and how it might be possible to achieve nuclear disarmament. Nuclear disarmament, if practicable, may well be a solution to the threats posed by nuclear weapons. But, a solution that cannot be put into practice is no solution—if not practicable, it is an illusion and potential distraction from paths that might actually be of help.

The prominent international relations scholar, Colin Gray, made this point four decades ago:

> How has one performed a noble service for peace,
> if he reminds people that "apocalypse now" is an
> ever-present possibility, tells them that there is a
> better world out there somewhere but lacks even
> the faintest glimmer of an half-way-plausible

theory concerning how we are to proceed from here to there?[30]

The Dilemma of Disarmament

A challenge confronting the realization of nuclear disarmament is that many states attribute great national security value to nuclear weapons. For example, some Russian commanders on the ground in Ukraine reportedly have argued that the only way Russia can prevail in this conflict is via the employment of nuclear weapons,[31] with winning described as replacing the Ukrainian government—presumably with one subservient to Moscow.[32] Russian Defense Minister Sergei Shoigu has emphasized that, "the nuclear shield has been and remains the main guarantor of the sovereignty and territorial integrity of our state."[33] And, former Russian President and current Deputy Chair of Russia's Security Council, Dmitry Medvedev, has observed that Russia's expansive nuclear arsenal is *the* factor that has deterred NATO from launching

---

[30] Colin S. Gray, "Nuclear Deterrence and the Catholic Bishops," *Information Series*, No. 140 (Fairfax, VA: National Institute, April 1983), p. 2.

[31] Andrew Stanton, "Russian Commander Suggests Nukes as 'Only' Option to Win War," *Newsweek Online*, December 13, 2022, available at https://www.newsweek.com/russian-commander-alexander-khodakovsky-suggests-nukes-only-option-win-ukraine-war-1766882.

[32] David Ljunggren, "Only Russia's nuclear arms preventing West from Declaring War - Putin Ally," December 25, 2022, *MSN.Com*, available at https://www.msn.com/en-us/news/world/only-russia-s-nuclear-arms-preventing-west-from-declaring-war-putin-ally/ar-AA15EZ4c?ocid=msedgdhp&pc=U531&cvid=b2ba92ef2baa4994be7c1d442f0681dd.

[33] Quoted in, "Russia to Keep Developing Nuclear Weapons, Defence Minister Says," *Reuters*, January 10, 2022, available at https://wifc.com/2023/01/10/russia-to-keep-developing-nuclear-weapons-defence-minister-says/.

a war against Russia in response to its invasion of Ukraine.[34] In short, Moscow shows by word and deed that it attributes enormous value to its nuclear arsenal for both expansionist and deterrence purposes.

Moscow is not alone in attributing great national security value to nuclear weapons. It is unsurprising that more than 30 countries, currently including the United States and the other members of the NATO alliance, highly value nuclear arms and deterrence to provide protection in a dangerous world, either through their own nuclear capabilities, or those of an alliance ally, notably the United States. Indeed, countries aspiring to become new members of NATO appear to seek alliance membership largely to secure the benefit of the U.S. extended nuclear "deterrence umbrella."[35]

America's Asian allies, including Japan and South Korea, also greatly value the U.S. extended nuclear deterrence umbrella for good reason—they face serious threats from powerful, threatening neighbors. Given North Korea's bellicosity and nuclear threats, South Korea increasingly seeks Washington's reassurance regarding the U.S. nuclear umbrella, and South Korean President Yoon Suk-yeol has now, for the first time, said that the North Korean nuclear threat may compel South Korea to acquire

[34] Ljunggren, "Only Russia's nuclear arms preventing West from Declaring War - Putin Ally," op. cit.

[35] "Russian Nuclear Threats Behind Finland NATO Move – Foreign Minister," *Kyodo News* (Japan), December 4, 2022, available at https://english.kyodonews.net/news/2022/12/e77d49b8e7ff-russian-nuclear-threats-behind-finland-nato-move-foreign-minister.html.

its own independent nuclear deterrent.[36] Japan frequently highlights the value it places on a credible U.S. nuclear umbrella, and, perhaps surprisingly, has refused to sign the recent international treaty initiative to ban nuclear weapons, has unveiled its largest military buildup since World War II, including the development of multiple missiles with ranges of up to 1,860 miles, and is reluctantly but rapidly moving away from its post-World War II pacifist constitution.[37]   These types of developments illustrate yet again the enduring power of security concerns to determine national behavior in an "anarchic" international system, including with regard to nuclear weapons.[38]

---

[36] See Choe Sang-Hun, "In a First, South Korea Declares Nuclear Weapons a Policy Option," *New York Times Online*, January 12, 2022, available at https://www.nytimes.com/2023/01/12/world/asia/south-korea-nuclear-weapons.html. See also the discussion in, Dasi Yoon, "South Korea Revives Nuclear Debate as Tensions With the North Rise Seoul Urges Washington to let it Play More Active Role in Nuclear-Weapons Management," *Wall Street Journal Online*, January 5, 2022, available at https://www.wsj.com/articles/south-korea-revives-nuclear-debate-as-tensions-with-the-north-rise-11672923760. See also, Park Jung-won, "South Korea needs its own nuclear deterrent," *Korea Times Online* (South Korea), December 1, 2022, available at https://koreatimes.co.kr/www/nation/2022/12/807_340930.html; and, Shim Jae-yun, "Consider all deterrence options," *Korea Times Online* (South Korea), November 16, 2022, available at https://www.koreatimes.co.kr/www/opinion/2022/11/197_339925.html.

[37] See, "The Sleeping Japanese Giant Awakes" *Wall Street Journal*, December 17, 2022, p. A14, available at https://www.wsj.com/articles/the-sleeping-japanese-giant-awakes-tokyo-defense-strategy-fumio-kishida-11671227810; and, Kantaro Komiya, "Japan to develop 3,000 km long-range missiles, deploy in 2030s – Kyodo," *Reuters*, December 31, 2022, available at https://www.reuters.com/business/aerospace-defense/japan-develop-3000-km-long-range-missiles-deploy-2030s-kyodo-2022-12-31/.

[38] The common use of the term "anarchic" to describe the international system is not to suggest that the system is devoid of any order, rules,

In short, U.S. allies either face serious security threats now, or understand that they may well face serious threats in the future; they highly value the U.S. nuclear deterrence extended on their behalf. This is not a new phenomenon; Winston Churchill lauded the role of nuclear weapons in World War II not for the destruction they caused, but because they averted "a vast, indefinite butchery" on all sides that would have occurred had Japan not surrendered and the war continued.[39] Allies well understand that another great power war fought to conclusion with contemporary *non-nuclear* weapons certainly would involve *far more* horrific "butchery" on all sides than that expected by Churchill in 1945. Deterring such a catastrophe now is a function of nuclear deterrence.

Of course, the United States also values nuclear deterrence for this purpose. For more than seven decades, Washington has relied on deterrence to help provide national security and the security of allies. On occasion, official enthusiasm for nuclear disarmament appears to have policy priority, but these initiatives are short lived.

President Jimmy Carter came into office asking why the U.S. strategic nuclear deterrent could not reside in a single ballistic missile-carrying submarine. He departed office having signed the "Countervailing Strategy," which was

---

norms or cooperation. It is to observe that there is no orderer with the apparent will or ability to enforce any set of global laws or cooperative behavioral norms reliably. Despite the common use of the phrase "international community," powerful states with aggressive ambitions ultimately can pursue their national goals *without* reliable external control or internal limits on their use of force to advance their aggressive ambitions. Their neighbors, near and far, ultimately are left to their own devices to protect themselves — the global order often is a merciless, "self-help" system. For a classic discussion of this anarchic context of international relations see, Hedley Bull, *The Anarchical Society* (New York: Columbia University Press, 1977), especially Part I.

[39] Winston Churchill, *Triumph and Tragedy* (New York: Bantam Books, 1962), p. 639.

the basis for the subsequent Reagan Administration's nuclear modernization program of the 1980s.

Two decades later, President Obama came into office vocally promoting global nuclear disarmament. Indeed, he was awarded the Nobel Prize for doing so. Nevertheless, he subsequently put into motion most of the current nuclear modernization program that now so alarms the nuclear disarmament community.

The Biden Administration's main nuclear policy document, the 2022 *Nuclear Posture Review* (NPR), carries on this tradition of a new presidential administration that enters with an apparent nuclear disarmament agenda, but, with time, moves toward general consistency with established bipartisan policy. The Biden Administration's NPR states: "Strategic deterrence remains a top priority mission for the Department of Defense (DoD) and the Nation. For the foreseeable future, nuclear weapons will continue to provide unique deterrence effects that no other element of U.S. military power can replace….[an] effective nuclear deterrent is foundational to broader U.S. defense strategy and the extended deterrence commitments we have made to allies and partners."[40]

The prospects for a global rejection of nuclear arms and deterrence present a dilemma for advocates of nuclear disarmament that they often ignore or too easily dismiss. As noted, the United States and dozens of other countries now rely on nuclear deterrence to help protect them against potentially existential threats from powerful neighbors. The critical question then is why these countries should reasonably be expected to reject the nuclear capabilities (U.S. or their own) that they are convinced are needed to support the nuclear deterrence policies necessary for their security in a dangerous international system? The dubious

---

[40] Department of Defense, *2022 Nuclear Posture Review*, October 2022, p. 12, available at https://media.defense.gov/2022/Oct/27/2003103845/-1/-1/1/2022-NATIONAL-DEFENSE-STRATEGY-NPR-MDR.PDF.p. 12.

presumption of many nuclear disarmament advocates appears to be that they are able to "educate" national leaders on the subject because they better understand the security needs of these countries than do those leaderships and thus can admonish them regarding the dangers of nuclear weapons and the lack of value that nuclear deterrence actually provides to their nations.

Nuclear disarmament advocates seemingly dismiss the reality that nuclear weapons do indeed pose a risk to survival for many, but *the lack of a nuclear deterrent* can also be seen as posing a risk to the survival of many. That disarmament advocates often seem not to recognize this fundamental point is illustrated by their frequent past claims that the United States should be particularly eager to pursue global nuclear disarmament because, given the U.S. advantages of conventional forces, U.S. power would be even more preponderant in a world *without* nuclear weapons.[41] Those advocates seem oblivious to the fact that this narrative regarding nuclear disarmament, i.e., it would advantage U.S. power, helped to ensure Russian and Chinese opposition to their disarmament agenda. Indeed, Russian President Putin reportedly viewed the U.S. nuclear disarmament push of the last decade "as just another U.S. trick to weaken his country,"[42] yet again demonstrating the continuing power of mistrust and security concerns to

[41] See for example, David Cortright and Raimo Värynen, *Towards Nuclear Zero* (London: International Institute for Strategic Studies, 2010), p. 19. See also, James Cartwright, Bruce Blair, et al., *Modernizing U.S. Nuclear Strategy, Force Structure and Posture, Global Zero US Nuclear Policy Commission Report* (Washington, D.C.: Global Zero, May 2012), available at http://www.globalzero.org/files/gz_us_nuclear_policy_commission_report.pdf.

[42] Quoted in, "Reviving Nuclear Arms Talks," December 15, 2008, available at http://gm5-lkweb.newscyclecloud.com/news/20081215/reviving-nuclear-arms-talks.

shape national perceptions and behavior. The problem, of course, was that "Nuclear abolition — as seen from Moscow, Beijing, Pyongyang — looked like a way to make the world safe for U.S. conventional strong-arm tactics."[43]

For global nuclear disarmament to become a reality, all pertinent states would need to decide to reject nuclear weapons and deterrence with the confident expectation that doing so would *not* leave them vulnerable to attack or extortion by opponents or prospective opponents. What that means in practice is that nuclear disarmament would have to occur near-simultaneously among the great powers and nuclear powers, with each state seriously trusting that its opponents and potential opponents would, in fact, give up their aggressive designs and nuclear capabilities, *along with any other capabilities that are a cause of deep apprehension* — possibly including chemical and biological weapons, and advanced conventional capabilities.

In short, the practicability of nuclear disarmament as an alternative solution to the threats posed by nuclear weapons depends on the plausibility that the threats, mistrust and insecurity that drive the need for nuclear deterrence can first largely be excised from international relations, with prevalent confidence that they will not return. In particular, the security fears that now drive states to seek nuclear deterrence protection would need to be resolved prior to a possibly prudent decision for nuclear disarmament, and leaders would have to have considerable confidence that serious security threats would not reemerge in the future. It is important to understand that those fears could not be fully resolved even if, somehow, global nuclear disarmament were to occur because states confront aggressors with other fearful, non-nuclear capabilities,

---

43 Paul Bracken, "Whatever Happened to Nuclear Abolition?" *The Hill*, March 19, 2019, available at https://thehill.com/opinion/national-security/434723-whatever-happened-to-nuclear-abolition.

including weapons of mass destruction, that would remain to threaten their survival. In the absence of the elimination of these other threats, nuclear disarmament alone would hardly solve the security fears that drive many states to seek a measure of protection via nuclear deterrence.

Disarmament advocates can exhort leaders that nuclear weapons are dangerously lethal, even "evil," but until the security fears that drive the felt need for nuclear deterrence are resolved, such admonitions will be unpersuasive to many leaders — most of whom are likely already well aware that nuclear weapons are dangerously lethal, which is why they are uniquely deterring. Disarmament is not a simplistic matter of "educating" leaders about the lethality of nuclear weapons and the risks associated with deterrence policies, as nuclear disarmament advocates seem to think. It is a matter of addressing the realities national leaders must confront, i.e., threats, mistrust, and insecurity, and the corresponding practical reasons that those leaders attribute great value to nuclear weapons and deterrence.

The fundamental considerations in this regard are not the lethality of nuclear weapons or the beauty of the vision of nuclear disarmament, but calculating which of these incompatible alternatives, nuclear disarmament or nuclear deterrence, can be deemed the more reasonable path to help mitigate national security fears. For states that do not or cannot exploit nuclear weapons and deterrence for their security, either because they see no need or because they have little or no capacity to acquire and sustain them, the rejection of deterrence in favor of nuclear disarmament may be an easy choice — nothing is lost and good will can be signaled. For those states that confront serious threats and attribute great value to nuclear deterrence, including for preserving their survival, the rejection of nuclear weapons and deterrence may appear to pose a greater risk than their preservation. Whether that perception is valid as an historical truth in each case and time is less important for the purposes of this discussion than the apparent fact that it is firmly held. That said, for some states, in some circumstances, the attribution of great value to nuclear weapons and deterrence almost certainly is accurate. Convincing national leaders whose countries are in these circumstances, or who believe that they are, to reject nuclear weapons and deterrence would be significant, but largely implausible for good reason.

The Real Problem

That dozens of countries place priority on nuclear deterrence and reject nuclear disarmament is not surprising. There is no international institution that can be counted on to come to their rescue if attacked. Allies can be unreliable, as has been demonstrated throughout history, and solemnly-signed international accords are violated with frequency and impunity—witness most recently Russia's 2014 and 2022 assaults on Ukraine despite Moscow's 1994 promise to respect Ukraine's sovereignty and territorial integrity and to refrain from the use of force against Ukraine.[44] The well-worn argument that nuclear weapons can be eliminated—if only leaders can be educated regarding the dangers of nuclear weapons and reach the enlightened consciousness needed to agree to eliminate them—ignores or misses the transformation of human behavior and international relations that would have to precede leaders of nuclear-armed states and their protected allies choosing disarmament. Leaderships that decide to acquire and retain nuclear weapons, and their protected allies, value those weapons for a logical, rational reason: In a world order in which national survival is at risk to aggressors who can attack as they will, many leaderships see nuclear capabilities as contributing to their countries'

---

[44] This commitment is contained in the 1994 Budapest Memorandum.

security in a way that is superior to relying on opponents' ultimate cooperation and reasonableness. This view is not without reason when a country faces powerfully-armed opponents or expects that it might do so.

States in the international system ultimately are "on their own" to preserve their survival. This truth has been demonstrated so many times in world history that it should be self-evident. Every century is filled with repeated examples of aggressors that attacked and devastated or eliminated neighboring countries because those aggressors sought to and were capable of doing so—no other power or institution had the will or capability to prevent them from doing so. Confidence cannot be attached to aggressors' promises of cooperation and restraint, and there is no international institution able reliably to control and discipline their behavior.

Consequently, until the corresponding fear and mistrust that compel countries to seek the means to protect themselves is removed from the international system, some countries, including the United States, will seek and be capable of acquiring the arms they believe are necessary to protect themselves, including nuclear weapons. That the United States and allies do so is neither immoral nor ignorant; they well understand the potential destructiveness of nuclear weapons and want to harness the deterrence effect thereof for their protection in a "self-help" international system in which fear and mistrust is endemic and survival ultimately often depends on the national power needed to deter or defeat an attacker. Nuclear weapons are not primarily the cause of that fear and mistrust—which exist for deeper reasons independent of nuclear weapons—they are a symptom of that well-earned fear, mistrust and insecurity.

This seemingly academic point is key to understanding why the global elimination of nuclear weapons requires first the transformation of the conditions of the international system that led to their creation and to their continuing development and deployment. Armaments, including nuclear arms, would likely be eliminated easily and cooperatively in an international system in which countries could confidently rely on their neighbors to be peaceful consistently by choice, or because they are compelled to be peaceful by a powerful, trustworthy authority that enforces the peace globally. That is, any real prospect for global nuclear disarmament will require the prior transformation from the existing international system in which fear and mistrust prevail because "the strong do what they can and the weak suffer what they must,"[45] to a system in which peace and security can be expected because would-be aggressors are reliably peaceful or controlled. And, of course, if even one great power decides it must have nuclear capabilities to help preserve its survival in a dangerous world, its opponents and potential opponents also will likely feel compelled to have nuclear protection. That is, as mentioned above, the choice to disarm would need to be virtually universal and simultaneous, at least among great powers — with each party confidently trusting that all others would choose to abide by such a decision, and that they would not subsequently become vulnerable to others' threats to their survival that are now addressed via nuclear deterrence. Rousing disarmament exhortation regarding the supposed immorality of nuclear weapons and deterrence cannot change this reality.

Unfortunately, the vision of international trust and amity is far from the reality of the past, the present, or the foreseeable future. Countries, for good reason, will not lay down their arms prior to the realization of that vision of trust and amity; nothing less is likely to provide the desired

---

[45] As the great ancient Greek historian and general Thucydides put it starkly in the Melian Dialogue. See Robert B. Strassler, ed., *The Landmark Thucydides: A Comprehensive Guide to the Peloponnesian War* (New York: Touchstone, 1996), p. 352.

condition of reliable international security and safety that would make disarmament a reasonable, prudent move. The vision is beautiful, but it cannot be assumed into existence as the basis for potentially life and death national policy decisions such as nuclear disarmament. This point is not in praise of nuclear weapons; it is in recognition of the real structural impediments to the potential for nuclear disarmament inherent in the international system.

In short, it is perhaps the most obvious characteristic of the "self-help" international system that because aggressors are not under reliable control, national power may be essential for national survival. Those advocates of nuclear disarmament who so easily, readily and often indignantly declare that all states must now give up their nuclear power because it is enormously destructive seem to ignore the obvious fact that, in an ultimately lawless international system, states acquire power because it can serve their cherished ends, including their survival. That states will seek and retain those capabilities deemed necessary for that purpose is a fully rational and moral national choice in an anarchic international system where survival is at risk.

The Security Dilemma and the Value of Nuclear Deterrence

As noted, nuclear weapons do indeed pose a real risk to survival, but the lack of a nuclear deterrent can also pose a risk to survival. There is considerable evidence that nuclear deterrence "works," at least on occasion, to prevent war or its escalation. From their meticulous research on U.S.-Soviet relations, Richard Lebow and Janice Stein conclude that nuclear deterrence moderated superpower behavior during the Cold War: "Once leaders in Moscow and Washington recognized and acknowledged to the other that a nuclear war between them would almost certainly lead to their mutual destruction....Fear of the consequences of nuclear war not only made it exceedingly improbable that either superpower would deliberately seek a military confrontation with the other; it made their leaders extremely reluctant to take any action that they considered would seriously raise the risk of war."[46] And, based on a careful examination of Soviet Politburo records, Russian historian Victor Gobarev concludes that America's unique nuclear deterrence capabilities "counterbalanced" Soviet local conventional superiority and were "the single most important factor which restrained Stalin's possible temptation to resolve the [1948-1949] Berlin problem by military means. Evidence obtained from [Soviet] oral history clearly supports this fact."[47]

Evidence of the deterring effect of nuclear weapons is not limited to U.S.-Soviet Cold War history. Considerable available evidence indicates that Saddam Hussein was deterred from the use of chemical and biological weapons in 1991 by U.S. nuclear deterrence.[48] And, General Shankar

[46] Richard Ned Lebow and Janice Gross Stein, *We All Lost the Cold War* (Princeton, NJ: Princeton University Press), 1994, p. 367.

[47] Victor Gobarev, "Soviet Military Plans and Actions During the First Berlin Crisis, 1948-1949," *Journal of Slavic Military Studies*, Vol. 10, No. 3 (September 1997), p. 5; and, James Acton, *Deterrence During Disarmament* (London: International Institute for Strategic Studies, March 2011), p. 34.

[48] Charles A. Duelfer, testimony, Senate Armed Services Committee, Subcommittee on Emerging Threats and Capabilities, *The Weapons of Mass Destruction Program of Iraq*, Senate Hearing 107-573, 107th Cong., 2nd Sess. (Washington, D.C.: GPO, 2002), pp. 92-93, available at http://frwebgate.access.gpo.gov/cgibin/getdoc.cgi?dbname=107_senate_hearings&docid=f:80791.pdf. See also the work by Kevin Woods, task leader of the Iraqi Perspectives Project at the Institute for Defense Analyses, and David Palkki, then Deputy Director of National Defense University's Conflict Records Research Center. They presented their respective views on this subject as described at a Policy Forum Luncheon by the Washington Institute for Near East Policy, "Knowing the Enemy: Iraqi Decisionmaking Under Saddam Hussein," September 20, 2010. This forum can be found at http://www.cspanarchives.org/program/id/233237.

Roychowdhury, India's former Army Chief, has observed that, "Pakistan's nuclear weapons deterred India from attacking that country after the Mumbai strikes" and, "it was due to Pakistan's possession of nuclear weapons that India stopped short of a military retaliation."[49] Historical evidence does *not* indicate that deterrence is infallible, but it is beyond doubt that nuclear weapons have contributed to the deterrence of war and escalation in the past.[50]

It is not difficult to understand that current Russian threats to employ nuclear weapons to end Western support for Ukraine would be much more fearsome did NATO not also have a nuclear deterrent to Russian attack. How many members of NATO would like to eliminate NATO nuclear capabilities in the context of an aggressive Russia that is incredibly well-armed with nuclear weapons and is brandishing nuclear threats on a seemingly daily basis? Did Russia's past solemn guarantees prevent its invasion of Ukraine or Moscow's subsequent stream of extreme nuclear threats? These threats have created greater concern about the probability of nuclear war than at any time in decades. Do the pertinent past disarmament agreements or *any others* now provide the much-appreciated measure of confidence that Moscow will *not* actually employ nuclear weapons, or do NATO's deterrence capabilities provide that comfort? It clearly is the latter; to answer that question is to identify the value of deterrence to prevent nuclear use.

Some Ukrainian leaders now understandably express regret over having given up the nuclear systems that had been located in Ukraine in return for Russia's now-

---

[49] Quoted in, "Pak's N-bomb prevented Indian retaliation after 26/11," *The Indian Express*, March 9, 2009, available at http://www.indianexpress.com/news/paks-nbomb-prevented-indian-retaliation-after-2611/432730/0.

[50] See the discussion in, Keith B. Payne and James Schlesinger, et al., *Minimum Deterrence: Examining the* Evidence (Fairfax, VA: National Institute Press, 2013), pp. 13-14.

worthless 1994 security guarantee. The power to deter attack is the value of nuclear weapons — a value that is not easily tossed aside for those countries at potential risk, or that could be at risk if they were unprotected, which includes many countries on Earth. Power, including nuclear power, may be needed in an international system that ultimately offers no other means of survival to those who are, or could be, under threat.[51]

Consequently, for many countries the elimination of nuclear deterrence could pose an existential threat. For these countries, it is not self-evident that this risk is less than that entailed by the continued existence of nuclear weapons; what is obvious is that not all countries that face this dilemma of competing risks will agree to disarm — not because they are foolish, ignorant or immoral, but because they fear the possibly horrific consequences of their disarming. That is not an unreasonable fear because some states do indeed face existential threats now, and others assuredly will in the future. The rhetoric of some nuclear disarmament advocates does not appear to recognize or appreciate this profound dilemma for countries that see themselves at risk or potential risk,[52] now including, for example, Russia's and China's neighbors and some former states of the Soviet Union that achieved independence following the Cold War.

---

[51] Hans Morgenthau, a well-known theorist from the Realist school of international relations, observed that the lawless character of the system drives national "interest defined as power." Hans Morgenthau, *Politics Among Nations: The Struggle for Power and Peace* (New York: Alfred Knopf, 1962), p. 5.

[52] In the midst of the Cold War, for example, Christian academic writers, Ronald Sider and Richard Taylor, advocated unilateral U.S. nuclear disarmament, stating, "it would seem imperative to call for a complete, unilateral and immediate renunciation of [nuclear] weapons." Ronald Sider and Richard Taylor, "International Aggression and Nonmilitary Defense," *Christian Century*, July 6-13, 1983, p. 644.

These reasons why the anarchic structure of the international system limits the prospect for cooperative global disarmament are not obscure, and have long been recognized in scholarly writings on international relations.[53] In a "self-help" global order, states that prioritize their survival often are constrained by that goal to policies that advance their national security and power, including, if necessary, at the expense of policies that would subordinate that goal for the purpose of international cooperation and amity. As University of Chicago Professor John Mearsheimer concludes, "States operating in a self-help world almost always act according to their own self-interest and do not subordinate their interests to the interests of other states, or to the interests of the so-called international community."[54]

Obviously, at least some states in the system are highly aggressive, past and present. They are willing to use force to achieve their aggressive goals and unwilling to adhere to cooperative norms. Periodically this includes great powers and catastrophic loss. Given their ambitions and methods, these states historically are *not* inclined to give up any real power cooperatively if they believe that power is key to their ambitions. Correspondingly, states concerned about potential aggression also are unlikely to give up any real power they deem necessary for their defense.

Even those leaders of states *without* aggressive designs and who earnestly seek an alternative to nuclear deterrence must be reluctant to engage in actual nuclear disarmament as the solution to their security fears because there is no reliable global body or international institution(s) to prevent others' aggression and enforce agreements and a

---

[53] The classic presentation of structural realism can be found in, Kenneth N. Waltz, *Man, the State and War* (New York: Columbia University Press, 1959).

[54] John J. Mearsheimer, *The Tragedy of Great Power Politics* (New York: W. W. Norton & Company, 2001), p. 33.

cooperative order. For example, at the high point of President Obama's promotion of global nuclear disarmament, he emphasized "America's commitment to seek the peace and security of a world without nuclear weapons." But, he also quickly added, "Make no mistake: as long as these weapons exist, we will maintain a safe, secure and effective arsenal to deter any adversary, and guarantee that defense to our allies."[55] This juxtaposition of competing goals, i.e., nuclear disarmament versus rearmament, was necessary because there is no basis for confidently expecting the absence of international aggression and violence — whether because states give up their aggressive ways by choice, or because they are compelled to do so by a powerful governing global authority.

Consequently, for nuclear disarmament, the prior necessary change in conditions includes the profound transformation of international relations and an enduring, consistent pattern of mutual trust, cooperation and non-violence in human behavior. Yet, these are the very characteristics absent from international relations, now and in the past. The transformation of the international system and in human behavior to reliable cooperation and mutual trust surely is to be welcomed by any sensible person, but that does not make the goal practicable. The needed transformation in the human condition and the global order that would have to take place for nuclear disarmament to be the obviously prudent choice cannot blithely be dismissed as an annoying detail, as so often seems to be the case. To call attention to such realities of an anarchic international system and nuclear disarmament is not to suggest favor for that structure or for nuclear weapons. It is to recognize the

---

[55] Department of State, U.S. Embassy in the Czech Republic, "President Obama's Speech in Prague," April 5, 2009, available at, https://cz.usembassy.gov/our-relationship/president-obamas-speech-in-prague/.

fundamental nature of that system and its implications for the usual tone and facile content of most church-based and secular nuclear disarmament advocacy.

The Past as Prelude

Unless a fundamental change in the long-existing world order takes place, along with an end to a seemingly permanent pattern of base human interactions, the removal of nuclear weapons from internal relations almost certainly would simply return the world to the *pre-nuclear* age, such as the first half of the 20th century in which up to 100 million lives were lost in two world wars and some countries were eliminated from existence. Indeed, the global elimination of nuclear weapons, were that possible, would not eliminate the underlying problems that have repeatedly led to great power wars in the past. In 2009, at the height of the "nuclear zero" political movement, Thomas Schelling, one of the 20th century's most renowned academic deterrence theorists and a Nobel laureate, offered this pertinent observation regarding the nuclear disarmament narrative:

> Why should we expect a world without nuclear weapons to be safer than one with (some) nuclear weapons? ...I have not come across any mention of what would happen in the event of a major war. One might hope that major war could not happen without nuclear weapons, but it always did....every responsible government must consider that other responsible governments will mobilize their nuclear weapons [production] base as soon as war erupts, or as soon as war appears likely, there will be at least covert frantic efforts, or perhaps purposely conspicuous efforts to acquire deliverable nuclear weapons as rapidly as possible. And what then?...The [existing] nuclear

quiet should not be traded away for a world in which a brief race to reacquire nuclear weapons could become every former nuclear state's overriding preoccupation.[56]

Professor Schelling's point, of course, is that unless the world order were transformed somehow, from anarchic to reliably cooperative, nuclear disarmament would not safeguard lives from horrific war, and could increase the dangers of such a war beyond those that *now* exist. He had made much the same point five decades earlier, observing that, in the absence of a cooperative new world order, "[Nuclear] disarmament would not preclude the eruption of a crisis; war and rearmament could seem imminent," and, "Short of universal brain surgery, nothing can erase the memory of weapons and how to build them...To suppose the contrary is to assume away the problem that disarmament is intended to solve..."[57]

Even if nuclear weapons were eliminated globally, given the existing technology for biological and chemical weapons, a new great power war could cause unprecedented loss of life, indeed, at levels comparable to a nuclear war. Nuclear disarmament could not preclude such a catastrophe whereas nuclear deterrence might help to do so. It is fashionable, but fallacious, to suggest that absent nuclear arms, there would not be the threat to humanity of horrific, unthinkable destruction. In fact, as Schelling suggested, nuclear disarmament could *increase* the probability of such a dreadful outcome. Why so? To the

---

[56] Thomas Schelling, "A World Without Nuclear Weapons?" *Daedalus* (Fall 2009), pp. 125-126, 129. Decades earlier, Schelling indicated his preference — in contrast to what he called "the 'ban the bomb' orientation" — is for deterrence to be viewed, "as something to be enhanced, not dismantled." See Thomas Schelling, *The Strategy of Conflict* (Cambridge, MA: Harvard University Press, 1960), p. 241.

[57] Thomas Schelling, "The Role of Deterrence in Total Disarmament," *Foreign Affairs*, Vol. 40, No. 3 (April 1962), pp. 393, 392, respectively.

extent that nuclear disarmament would remove the nuclear deterrent barrier to war, but not eliminate the chemical, biological or advanced conventional weapons that could be used in war, nuclear disarmament could actually increase the prospects for unprecedented levels of human and material loss.   Again, nuclear disarmament activists generally appear not even to wrestle with this problem, seemingly assuming wrongly that, somehow, these other threats have disappeared or that nuclear deterrence is irrelevant to countering those threats — neither of which is a reasonable assumption.

Given the harsh reality of international relations, the need for power in a self-help system is not a paranoid perception; it is a reasonable response by those burdened with responsibility for national security and has been so for all of recorded history. The frequent rhetoric of those who advocate for nuclear disarmament offers no solution to this reality that drives many countries to see nuclear weapons as a necessary tool of deterrence and survival. This view is not a result of malevolence or ignorance; it follows from centuries of world history that demonstrate that fear and mistrust in the international system is reasonable and to be expected. It is this enduring fear and mistrust that must be replaced by reliable, enduring cooperation and trust before disarmament can be the obviously prudent choice for all.

Those civilian and military officials with serious national security responsibilities and experience generally, if not always, understand this reality of international relations and its implications for the prospects for disarmament. They rightly place a priority on national survival and the means they believe are needed for survival. Doing so shapes their thinking in ways that appear inexplicable and foreign to those who have not shared such responsibilities. Sir Michael Howard, the late, highly regarded Oxford professor (who also had pertinent senior government experience), observed that those with serious national security responsibilities "share a common skepticism as to the possibility of disarmament or indeed of the creation of any effective international authority to whom they can turn over any portion of their authority." To this keen observation, Sir Michael added that "the impatient onlookers, who have never themselves been plunged into that element, cannot understand why."[58]

Indeed, some advocates of a global transformation without such experience believe their goal is so self-evidently reasonable that the lack of progress can only be explained as the result of the workings of some willful obstructionist forces, including "Our common-law tradition, a penchant for philosophical pragmatism and operationalism, and the dominance of Protestant forms of worship...,"[59] "a handful of willful [U.S.] senators who choose to pursue their narrow, selfish political objectives...[and] pander to and are supported by the Christian Coalition,"[60] and an American media that supposedly "exclude advocates of nuclear disarmament or opponents of violent geopolitics."[61] It is, perhaps, ironic that some secular advocates identify Christian organizations and "forms of worship" as the villains in their narrative when the latter's application of the Just War Doctrine often leads to the same general conclusions regarding disarmament and deterrence.

Disarmament advocates occasionally object to the notion that global nuclear disarmament likely is impracticable absent global transition by asserting that the international community already has demonstrated the

[58] Michael Howard, *Studies in War and Peace* (New York: Viking Press, 1964), pp. 215-216.
[59] Richard Falk, *This Endangered Planet* (New York: Vintage Books, 1971), p. 290.
[60] World Federalist Association, "Cronkite Champions World Government," *Washington Times*, December 3, 1999, p. A2.
[61] Falk in, *The Path to Zero*, op. cit., p. 160.

capacity for global, transformative change:　It has eliminated slavery and has banned chemical and biological weapons; the same global enlightened reason should similarly work to ban nuclear weapons cooperatively.[62] But, it is not quibbling in this regard to point out that the horror of slavery in the United States was not ended cooperatively, but only following the cataclysmic Civil War, and that slavery still exists globally on an unprecedented scale,[63] and that the international agreements intended to eliminate chemical and biological weapons have clearly failed in some cases,[64] and appear likely to have failed in other cases, notably including China and Russia.[65]

In the immediate aftermath of the Cold War, expectations of a cooperative "New World Order" led to widespread Western optimism regarding nuclear

---

[62] "In certain respects, the challenge of abolishing nuclear weapons has some similarities to the challenge of abolishing slavery that took place in the last century.　It appeared to be an almost hopeless goal at some point in time and yet we were able as a species and as specific societies to meet that moral challenge."　David Krieger, in "Where We Stand:　A Dialogue," in, *At the Nuclear Precipice*, Richard Falk and David Krieger, eds. (New York:　Palgrave Macmillan, 2008), p. 245.

[63] "Modern slavery occurs in almost every country in the world and cuts across ethnic, cultural and religious lines." United Nations, *50 Million People in Modern Slavery: UN Report*, September 27, 2022, available at https://www.un.org/en/delegate/50-million-people-modern-slavery-un-report.

[64] See for example, U.S. Department of State, "OPCW Condemns Syria's Repeated Use of Chemical Weapons, *Media Note*, April 22, 2021, available at https://www.state.gov/opcw-condemns-syrias-repeated-use-of-chemical-weapons/.

[65] See the discussion in, Department of Defense, *2022 Nuclear Posture Review*, pp. 4, 9, 10, available at https://news.usni.org/2022/10/27/2022-national-defense-strategy-nuclear-posture-review.　See also, Department of Defense, *Military and Security Developments Involving the People's Republic of China*, 2022, p. X, available at, https://media.defense.gov/2022/Nov/29/2003122279/-1/-1/1/2022-MILITARY-AND-SECURITY-DEVELOPMENTS-INVOLVING-THE-PEOPLES-REPUBLIC-OF-CHINA.PDF.

disarmament, including by some otherwise nuclear realists.[66] Yale Professor Paul Bracken observes of this time: "All were on board to oppose nuclear arms....Academics, think tanks and intellectuals quickly jumped on the bandwagon. For a time, it really looked like there was going to be an antinuclear turn in U.S. strategy."[67]

Yet, after fewer than 20 years, those optimistic expectations have been shattered again by another cycle of great power conflicting interests and mounting hostility. While in much of the world there has been obvious, great technological progress, including in global communications, transportation, food production, materials and medicine, there again is little if any indication that the mistrust, enmity and proclivity to conflict prevalent in international relations is abating—indeed, these characteristics that drive national security fears and the need for arms seem to be intensifying dangerously

This repetition of past cycles of international animosity and conflict has come as no surprise to some scholars with an appreciation of history. In 1999, Professor Colin Gray dismissed then-prevalent expectations of a more cooperative New World Order and pointed to "the strong possibility that world politics two to three decades hence will be increasingly organized around the rival poles of U.S. and Chinese power," and that China then "would menace Japan." He also fully expected that Russia would again confront the West militarily and "immediately would

---

[66] See for example, George P. Shultz, William J. Perry, Henry A. Kissinger, and Sam Nunn, "A World Free of Nuclear Weapons," *The Wall Street Journal*, January 4, 2007, available at https://www.wsj.com/articles/SB116787515251566636; and, George P. Shultz, William J. Perry, Henry A. Kissinger, and Sam Nunn, "Toward a Nuclear-Free World," *The Wall Street Journal*, January 15, 2008, available at https://www.wsj.com/articles/SB120036422673589947.
[67] Bracken, "Whatever Happened to Nuclear Abolition?" op. cit.

threaten independent Ukraine [and] the Baltics."[68]   As
Professor Gray forecast, the immediate post-Cold War
period, with its short-lived burst of optimism for
international amity and nuclear disarmament, was but a
brief interlude before a return to sharp great power hostility
and conflict.

The Transformation of the World Order

Given the apparently enduring anarchic character of the
international system, and the corresponding, seemingly
enduring reality of periodic uncontrolled aggression, the
admonition that all states should move to nuclear
disarmament will, understandably, fail to convince at least
some leaderships until there is a reliable answer to the
following question: If nuclear weapons and nuclear
deterrence are to be rejected, what then is to deter, or
otherwise protect against aggressors that have violent
intentions and are armed with nuclear weapons, possibly
chemical   and   biological   weapons,   and/or   with
overwhelming conventional capabilities?   U.S. allies and
partners now bordering Russia, North Korea or Iran, or
facing a militarized, expansionist China, are likely to be
particularly keen on a serious, practicable answer.

Some disarmament advocates duly recognize this
dilemma, but reply, "These are valid points, but they do not
diminish the necessity of disarmament. Acknowledgement
of fundamental security realities makes nuclear
disarmament more, not less, urgent. Reliance on deployed
nuclear weapons as a form of deterrence is an imperfect
security strategy, not least because it validates the utility of
the weapons and spurs proliferation."[69] Indeed, deterrence

---

[68] Colin S. Gray, *The Second Nuclear Age* (London: Lynn Reiner Press,
1999), pp. 39-41.
[69] Cortright and Värynen, *Towards Nuclear Zero*, op. cit., p. 20.

is "an imperfect security strategy"; it can fail. But, in an anarchic international system perfect and infallible options are not available and simply doubling down on expressing the need for disarmament does not suggest how it becomes a practicable alternative.

Particularly unhelpful in this regard is the proffered answer, found in some form in virtually all advocacy of nuclear disarmament, that when an unprecedented level of international cooperation becomes the norm in international relations—when major international conflicts of interest can be resolved more cooperatively—then disarmament will become "feasible." For example, "To build confidence that an agreement to prohibit nuclear weapons would be enforced, all states would need to demonstrate a willingness to enforce international rules with greater alacrity and robustness than has been historically normal."[70]   And, when the "tensions and animosities that lead nations to fear their neighbors have declined towards zero," there may well be no "desire or need to possess nuclear weapons."[71]   That suggestion is likely true; if those happy conditions ever were to prevail reliably, there obviously would be little need for arms, including nuclear arms, to protect against aggression. If and when conflicts of interest leading to international friction, current and future, can reliably be resolved peacefully—if nations can just learn to "enforce rules" more cooperatively and peacefully—radical disarmament would be possible and prudent because a new reality will have arrived.

[70] George Perkovich and James Acton, *Abolishing Nuclear Weapons, Adelphi Papers*, No. 396 (London: International Institute for Strategic Studies, 2008), p. 9. See also, Falk and Krieger, *The Path to Zero*, op. cit., pp. 208-209; and, Richard Falk, "Nuclear Weapons, War, and the Discipline of International Law," in, *At the Nuclear Precipice*, Falk and Krieger, eds., op. cit., pp. 225-233.
[71] Cortright and Värynen, *Towards Nuclear Zero*, op. cit., p. 21.

Unfortunately, that observation is easy to make and often is presented as if it were profound guidance for the global elimination of nuclear weapons. But that frequent observation is as obvious as it is useless — akin to saying that were there a general cure for cancer, treatments would be unnecessary, or were all humans reliably pacifists, there would be no need for police or national armaments to deter and defend. Both are truisms and beautiful hopes that undoubtedly have been expressed for thousands of years. But they provide no useful guidance regarding the practicability of realizing those hopes. National policies cannot be based on the expectation that a general cure for cancer is forthcoming, that all humans will become reliable pacifists, or that international relations will become reliably cooperative in any predictable time frame.

Instead, considerable evidence suggests that friction points and the potential for conflict flowing from irreconcilable national interests and goals have been and are consistently present in the international system; moreover, they show no sign of abating. Currently, for example, Moscow believes that recovering control of Ukraine — directly or indirectly — and incorporating at least parts of Ukrainian territory within Russian borders is its just prerogative and an existential goal.[72] President Putin describes Moscow's unprovoked attacks and occupation of Ukrainian territory as follows: "I believe that we are acting in the right direction, we are defending our national

---

[72] See the discussion in, Michael Schwirtz, Anton Troianovski, Yousur Al-Hlou, Masha Froliak, Adam Entous and Thomas Gibbons-Neff, "Putin's War," *New York Times*, December 18, 2022, p. A1, available at https://www.nytimes.com/interactive/2022/12/16/world/europe/ru ssia-putin-war-failures-ukraine.html.

interests, the interests of our citizens, our people. And we have no other choice but to protect our citizens."[73]

Ukraine, however, shows by word and deed that it believes it has the just prerogative to defend itself against Russian attack and preserve its independence from Moscow. This too is an existential goal. Reconciliation in this case may be possible, but at this point it does not appear likely until one side has essentially achieved its goal or given it up, or one or both sides are too exhausted to continue the battle. However this particular case may resolve in time, unless there is a profound transformation of international relations, one or more cases of irreconcilable differences leading to the use of force will be forthcoming. The ultimately banal observation that when this cycle comes to an end disarmament will be possible is unhelpful because conflicting self-justifications and perceptions of existential goals, and a willingness to use force brutally to achieve those goals, is not unusual in international relations — it is a lamentable norm that has been present throughout known history.

In short, knowingly observing that when international relations can be rendered reliably amicable, the problem of nuclear armaments and war can be resolved is the pretense of a useful answer. It simply redirects the question to asking how it might be possible to realize an international system in which the great conflicts of interest and friction points are resolved reliably and cooperatively to the satisfaction of all. *How* does that new norm become consistent, reliable practice for the first time in known history? The popular 1969 song "Woodstock" by noted singer/songwriter Joni

---

[73] Quoted in Gerrard Karonga, "Russian TV Warns 'Big War' Coming After Putin Ultimatum," *msn.com*, January 23, 2023, available at https://www.msn.com/en-us/news/world/russian-tv-warns-new-big-war-coming-after-putin-ultimatum/ar-AA16EhGT?ocid=msedgdhp&pc=U531&cvid=44c726a2bc354e95b4ec5a0c4f7cecd4.

Mitchell laments the thought of bombers overhead and concludes that humanity must get itself "back to the garden" (presumably the Garden of Eden). The dowdy realist says, "yes indeed, a wonderful sentiment, but realistically, how do we get from here to there?"

To the extent that the "how to" question is addressed by secular and church-based disarmament advocates, their common answer is suggested by the American Catholic Bishops' 1983 report. It identifies nuclear possession and deterrence as interim measures that are conditionally acceptable until nuclear weapons can be fully eliminated under the watchful and benign governance of a "global body" that establishes and enforces "a substitute for war." The report describes this as a "global body" that is able to provide "supervision" for disarmament worldwide, and is equipped "to keep constant surveillance on the entire earth," has "the authority, freely conferred upon it by all the nations, to investigate what seems to be preparation for war by any one of them," and is, "empowered by all the nations to enforce its commands on every nation."[74]   The problematic words "world government" are avoided in the report, but the "global body" described obviously is a form of benign and powerful world governor.   Methodist Bishops, in their 1986 report, similarly point to nuclear disarmament via some form of global institution endowed with "effective authority to assure common security..."[75]

Professor Schelling observed five decades ago that such a global body would have to be enormously powerful to carry out the task of prescribing and enforcing disarmament: "Some kind of international authority is generally proposed as part of an agreement on total [nuclear] disarmament. If militarily superior to any

[74] Catholic Bishop's Pastoral Letter, "The Challenge of Peace: God's Promise and Our Response," op. cit., p. 30.
[75] United Methodist Church, Council of Bishops, *In Defense of Creation: The Nuclear Crisis and a Just Peace*, op. cit., p. 71 (Foundation Document).

combination of national forces, an international force implies (or is) some form of world government"; it would need to have the capability to "meet large-scale aggression."[76] For Schelling, the prospect of such a body was more foreboding than assuring: "We may achieve it if we create a sufficiently potent and despotic ruling [global] force; but then some of us would have to turn around and start plotting civil war..."[77] The theoretical problem, of course, is that any such global body run and staffed by humans would be subject to human patterns of behavior, including inconsistency, aggression, oppression, injustice, and a lack of trustworthiness. These may *not* be inherent in human nature, but they are characteristics that appear to be enduring, including not infrequently in the behavior of leaders and in the institutions they govern.

Yet, *many* church-based *and* secular advocates of nuclear disarmament have long- identified some form of a powerful "global body," international institution(s) and/or transnational cooperative legal system as the means to achieve the transformation of the world order and nuclear disarmament.[78] Article 4, Paragraph 1 of the Treaty on the Prohibition of Nuclear Weapons, for example, calls for a new "competent international authority" and "safeguards" agreements "sufficient to provide credible assurance of the

---

[76] Schelling, "The Role of Deterrence in Total Disarmament," op. cit., pp. 401, 403.

[77] Ibid, p. 405.

[78] See for example, Jonathan Schell, *The Fate of the Earth* (New York: Alfred Knopf, 1982), especially Part 3; see also, Ashton Carter, William Perry, and John Steinbruner, *A New Concept of Cooperative Security* (Washington, D.C.: Brookings Institution, January 1992), pp. 11, 24, 30, 35, 59, 63; Roger Speed, *The International Control of Nuclear Weapons* (Stanford, CA: Center for International Security and Arms Control, 1994); Perkovich and Acton, *Abolishing Nuclear Weapons*, op. cit., pp. 100-102, 110; Falk, *This Endangered Planet*, op. cit., Chapters 7 and 8; Krieger, "Where We Stand: A Dialogue," op. cit., p. 208; and, World Federalist Association, "Cronkite Champions World Government," op. cit., p. A2.

non-diversion of declared nuclear material from peaceful nuclear activities and of the absence of undeclared nuclear material or activities..."   Paragraph 6 calls on this "competent international authority or authorities to negotiate and verify the irreversible elimination of nuclear weapons programs..."[79]

The logic of this argument for disarmament through a transformation of the global order is presented concisely by Professor Lawrence Wittner:

> If the roots of the nuclear problem lie in a pathological national-state system, then we need to do no more (and should do no less) than change that system. Some of the necessary changes have been recognized for a century or more. Foremost among them is strengthening international authority so that it can provide an effective system of security for all nations. This process was begun with the creation of the League of Nations and the United Nations....if citizens' movements can force nations to follow through on creating an effective international security organization, they can pull the deadly fangs of the nation-state system.[80]

The general proposition here is that under the auspices and discipline of a reliable global authority or international institution(s), a new international order and nuclear disarmament will be able to flourish. The contemporary anarchic system is somehow to be replaced by a new international system that is governed by a benevolent international regime able to create and enforce rules, eliminate or control nuclear weapons, and provide all nations a large measure of security against aggression—

---

[79] United Nations, *Treaty on the Prohibition of Nuclear Weapons*, op. cit.

[80] Lawrence Wittner, *The Struggle Against the Bomb, Volume Three: Toward Nuclear Abolition* (Stanford, CA: Stanford University Press, 2003), pp. 490-491.

thus also eliminating the need and rationale for the possession of nuclear weapons and deterrence by individual states.

In this regard, the 2009 report of the Congressional Strategic Posture Commission (the Perry-Schlesinger Commission) rightly observed that, "The conditions that might make possible the global elimination of nuclear weapons are not present today and their creation would require a fundamental transformation of the world political order."[81]

There is no doubt that a new peaceful world order governed by a benevolent, reliable and powerful global body or institution(s) would be much preferable to the current anarchic order that has existed for all recorded history. The existence of such a global body would essentially change the basic nature of the international system—replacing the current, anarchic and war-prone system with a new peaceful order enforced by a reliable, powerful global authority. Some church-based and secular advocates of disarmament offer a description of this global body, occasionally in minute detail.[82]

Those disarmament advocates who address the practical question of how to create the conditions needed for nuclear disarmament by pointing to some form of powerful international governance essentially respond to the Strategic Posture Commission's observation regarding the need for a new world order by explaining that the existing international system can be transformed to make disarmament a reality. But, pointing to any form of benign and powerful global order and orderer as the solution,

---

[81] Congressional Commission on the Strategic Posture of the United States, *America's Strategic Posture* (Washington, D.C.: U.S. Institute of Peace, 2009), p. xvi.

[82] For the classic description see, Grenville Clark and Louis Sohn, *World Peace Through World Law* (Cambridge, MA: Harvard University Press, 1960).

again, is not a serious answer to the question of how disarmament becomes practicable. It simply avoids that question and then leaves unexplained how and why such a new global authority that can prescribe and enforce disarmament should be expected to come into being in the foreseeable future when, by all evidence, such a transformation has not occurred in all history, and *not* for a lack of serious effort. Proposals for and descriptions of the new order and orderer typically side-step the all-important question of identifying and explaining the unprecedented dynamic that will effectively drive the international system from mistrust and anarchy to a trusting, cooperative, controlled order. If that dynamic cannot be explained and its transformative power is not readily apparent, national leaders can hardly be expected to dispose of capabilities they deem critical for their national security; doing so would neither be rational nor prudent.

There have been multiple efforts over centuries to create a new international system in which peace is protected and disarmament is enforced by global institutions. Most obvious in this regard are the League of Nations after World War I and the United Nations following World War II. Both the League of Nations and the United Nations were established with the hope and expectation of a new peaceful international order under international law and governance. As renowned religious scholar and Georgetown University Professor William O'Brien observes, "The age of Wilson and the League of Nations sought to replace the discredited [international] system that had brought World War I with a new system based on international law and organization. This idealist approach expected that nations could be persuaded to renounce the war system in exchange for new international institutions for settlement of disputes, backed up by collective security."[83]

However, both of these attempts consistently failed to provide the intended international trust, security and order needed for international security, peace, or disarmament. Brian Urquhart, then-General Undersecretary of the United Nations, remarked at the festive ceremonies celebrating the U.N.'s fortieth anniversary, that the needed genuine unity and agreement within the U.N. to make that promise real will not be possible "until an invasion from Mars takes place."[84] The former U.S. Ambassador to the U.N., John Bolton, more recently made a similar observation, noting that unity and agreement within the U.N. will come when, "unicorns break free and sweetness and light prevails."[85] These humorous quips capture a critical truth, i.e., a powerful dynamic not yet seen or experienced will be needed to drive the international cooperation, trust and unity necessary to create and sustain a reliable, powerful and benign global orderer. To present a convincing case, nuclear disarmament advocates need to identify and elaborate on that dynamic that will perform the functional equivalent of Urquhart's "invasion from Mars."

The Proposed Dynamics Driving Global Transformation

The fundamental question that must be addressed then is not *whether* a benign, reliable and powerful global body that

---

[83] O'Brien, *The Conduct of Just and Limited War*, op. cit., p. 209.

[84] Quoted in George Spieker, Deutsche Presse-Agentur, "Einigkeit in der UNO erst bei einer Invasion vom Mars," *Washington Journal*, July 15, 1985, p. 1.

[85] Quoted in, Ashley Semier, "Why Isn't the UN Doing More to Stop What's Happening in Ukraine?" *CNN*, April 15, 2022, available at https://www.cnn.com/2022/04/15/politics/united-nations-ukraine-russia/index.html.

would judiciously enforce rules and a cooperative world order would be far superior to the current anarchic, war-torn international system. That much is self-evident and not in dispute here. Nor is it difficult to describe that hoped-for order and orderer in theory. Indeed, numerous academic texts and futuristic books and cinema show such a system functioning. The fundamental question, however, is why/how should it be expected that humankind will now be able to transition to an international order in which peace flourishes under a benign and powerful global authority or international institution(s), and nations can thereby prudently choose to disarm? Again, what is the dynamic that now makes that transition a reality when it has not occurred to this point in history?

The general answers to that question offered by church-based and secular advocates of nuclear disarmament typically are vague, obscure, and/or transcendental.[86] For example, nuclear disarmament can be a "black swan phenomenon" that "consists of those parts of reality that shape historical change but are currently hidden from our perception or understanding..."[87] Momentum for disarmament "calls on every person to disarm his or her own heart and to be a peacemaker everywhere....personal and communal conversion and change of heart."[88] And, "When it becomes possible, it will be as a result of the intervention in our history of some totally unanticipated happening: a shock of some sort to the system, a charismatic leader who mobilizes a new public consciousness, a new cultural turn toward spirituality and

---

[86] "At bottom, effective opposition to nuclear deterrence must be rooted in morality, law, and a sense of the spiritual destiny and potential of the human species." Richard Falk in, Falk and Krieger, *The Path to Zero*, op. cit., p. 36.

[87] Ibid, pp. 200, 204.

[88] Peter Turkson, "Foreword," in, *A World Free from Nuclear Weapons: The Vatican Conference on Disarmament*, op. cit., pp. x-xi.

universal humanism, even a repudiation of war as a legitimate institution."[89]

Perhaps these descriptions of how a transformation of the anarchic global order can take place are prescient. But, leaderships responsible for their nations' security cannot prudently make the potentially life and death decision that their nations disarm on the basis of "some totally unanticipated happening," "a new cultural turn toward spirituality and universal humanism," a "black swan phenomenon," or on widespread "personal and communal conversion." This is not to state that such developments are impossible, but that they are, at best, opaque and unpredictable on any anticipated time frame; they can hardly be the basis for prudent national security planning and decisions by leaders continually confronting national security threats in an anarchic international system.

The proposition often presented essentially is that the desired transition in the global order needed for disarmament can be the result of an ongoing trend in human progress and reason.[90] This suggestion is consistent with the prevalent Western notion that international relations and human progress in general are on a trajectory towards enlightened cooperation. As Columbia University Professor Richard Betts, observes: "Most U.S. citizens view international relations through the prism of the liberal tradition, which emphasized the idea of progress from primitive conflict toward enlightened cooperation, a view reinforced by the end of the Cold War. Progress [according to this view] should obviate the quest for instruments of

---

[89] Falk, in *The Path to Zero*, op. cit., p. 201.

[90] Examples of cooperation and progress can be enumerated: "...optimism is the most logical, sound, and defensible position to arrive at after a rigorous study of history. We do not live in a perfect world. *But we live in a perfectible one.* History shows that, over the long run, we collectively have made progress work." David Rothkopf, "The Case for Optimism," *Foreign Policy*, No. 221 (Nov.-Dec. 2016), p. 56. (Emphasis added).

mass killing, not spur it."[91] Progress is expected on a trajectory toward the condition of enlightened and unprecedented cooperation.

The American Catholic Bishops in their 1983 Pastoral Letter correspondingly identify the power of "public opinion" and "the genius of man" as dynamics for the needed progress and transformation of the global order.[92] Others suggest that "revolutions of the mind," "rising powers in the non-West" and "countries that embrace soft power" can drive national "accountability" under "international law," "the needed nonviolent revolution," and thus a "peace-centric system." These, it is said, can lead "toward peace" and the needed global transformation and disarmament.[93] Additional factors identified decades ago as the dynamic for this transformation are, "a lot of courage, a lot of faith in the new order,"[94] "a sense of urgency," "human consciousness," and "action…grounded on a solid foundation of hope." These can lead to "change so profound that the status of man himself is drawn into question…"[95] The end of the Cold War encouraged optimism that a general fear of nuclear weapons could be the needed dynamic and that because of "the unipolar nature of international power," i.e., U.S. ascendency, "It is difficult to think of any moment since the height of the Roman empire in which the establishment of a world state was more possible than now."[96]

---

[91] Richard K. Betts, "Universal Deterrence or Conceptual Collapse? Liberal Pessimism and Utopian Realism," in, Victor Utgoff, ed., *The Coming Crisis* (Cambridge, MA: MIT Press, 2000), p. 51.

[92] "The Challenge of Peace: God's Promise and Our Response," op. cit., p. 30.

[93] Falk and Krieger, *The Path to Zero*, op. cit., pp. 208-209.

[94] "Cronkite Champions World Government," op. cit., p. A2.

[95] Falk, *This Endangered Planet*, op. cit., pp. 292-293.

[96] Campbell Craig, *Glimmer of a New Leviathan* (New York: Columbia University Press, 2003), pp. 171-172.

More recently, various commentators, including Nobel laureates, identify the need for, "people in all sectors of society to work hard and to work together to make that vision a reality."[97] Additional potential dynamics recently identified include, "the normative force of the prohibition of acquiring nuclear weapons," the common desire for nuclear non-proliferation and existing treaty obligations under the Nuclear Non-Proliferation Treaty, and "unofficial advance work " done "by international experts."[98]

Perhaps human genius, reason and progress, hard work, a new public consciousness, hope, faith, courage, revolutions of the mind, world public opinion, the fear of nuclear weapons and proliferation, non-Western powers, and international experts, *inter alia*, can be the engines that drive the cooperative transformation of human behavior and international relations. But, to risk understatement, given all the power attributed to these dynamics, it is untenable that the *why, how* and *when* they should be expected to do so remains clouded in ambiguity, an unresolved mystery.

Given the centrality of this pending global transformation to nuclear disarmament advocacy, the absence of such a transition in all of history, and the potentially serious security implications of abandoning nuclear deterrence, an examination of the proposition is warranted. Again, how/why would it be reasonable to base security policy decisions on the expectation that these suggested dynamics will become so powerful that they drive a cooperative transition at a foreseeable point in history? To pose these questions is not to scorn the beauty

---

[97] Nobel laureate Jody Williams, "Essay: Will Russia use tactical nukes? It's time to abolish nuclear weapons," *Houston Chronicle*, November 6, 2022, available at
https://www.houstonchronicle.com/opinion/outlook/article/Russia-tactical-nuclear-weapons-nobel-peace-prize-17558465.php.
[98] Perkovich and Acton, op. cit., pp. 7-8, 13, 84.

of the vision, but to probe whether prudent national security decisionmakers can base their efforts on the hope/expectation that public opinion, human reason, genius, progress, hard work, etc. will indeed drive and sustain the needed transition of the global order and, correspondingly, enable nuclear disarmament.

For example, human reason and world "public opinion" have long been identified as the key factors to transform the global order. The renowned historian E.H. Carr described this popular proposition after World War I: "Reason could demonstrate the absurdity of the international anarchy; and with increasing knowledge, enough people would be rationally convinced of its absurdity to put an end to it."[99] Indeed, President Woodrow Wilson's vision for the League of Nations following World War I was built on the notion that world public opinion would empower that global body to have a reliable restraining effect on otherwise aggressive states.[100]

Yet, of course, the hopes and expectations that reason and world public opinion, expressed through the League of Nations, would be the dynamic and vehicle for ending the anarchic global order were dashed in little more than a decade after its 1920 founding by the enduring realities of competing national interests, irreconcilable national goals and the brutal use of force leading to World War II. Hans Morgenthau explained this failure of world public opinion to perform as hoped by noting that world public opinion could not be harnessed to prevent aggression prior to or after World War II. He labeled as folly the appeal to world public opinion as the dynamic for profound change because the existence of a knowable, unified and actionable world public opinion "is not supported by the facts." Rather, "all the antagonists in the international arena believe

[99] Edward Hallett Carr, *The Twenty Years' Crisis, 1919-1939* (New York: Harper and Row, 1964), p. 26.
[100] Ibid., pp. 8-18, 27-36.

themselves to be supported by world public opinion…[all] people want to believe that they champion not only, and perhaps not even primarily, their own national interests but the ideas of humanity as well."[101]   Indeed, James Stoessinger, a noted academic historian and U.N. official, demonstrated in his century-spanning case studies how all leaderships tend to see their goals and related decisions to use force as right and justified.[102]

The practicality of public opinion as the proposed powerful dynamic for change was and remains problematic; the reasons why this is true are not complicated. For it to fulfill the proposed role, fundamental *unanswered* questions would have to be answered to the satisfaction of those responsible for national security: What is world public opinion?   Who defines it and on what universally accepted basis? Why should public opinion now be expected to be unified worldwide as opposed to conflicting, and how is it to have a common effect on the policies of susceptible democratic and less susceptible totalitarian leaderships to compel their cooperative resolution of conflicting national interests—rather than being a driver of diverse, competing national goals and conflict? Assuming for the moment that a world public opinion exists, can be defined, and is coherent, what universally accepted institution is to enforce it reliably? How is it to be harnessed to be the powerful dynamic that changes the international order, and what is the compelling evidence that this is feasible?   As a tool of human institutions, why should national leaders *not* expect that world public opinion would be defined and promoted to the benefit of some and the disadvantage of others? Why should the human institution defining and promoting

---

[101] Morgenthau, *Politics Among Nations*, op. cit., pp. 261-269, 271.

[102] James Stoessinger, *Why Nations Go to War* (Belmont, CA: Thomas Wadsworth, 2008), pp. XV, 385-411. Reportedly, 71% of the Russian public supports Russia's war on Ukraine.

public opinion be trusted to do so in such a way that all nations are protected and benefited?

Until these questions, and more, are realistically answered with confidence and manifest evidence, easily pointing to public opinion as the dynamic for global transformation will remain a superficial answer to the question of what, realistically, is the dynamic for the transformation of the global order. To risk understatement, these questions remain unanswered despite the transformative power that has been ascribed to public opinion. Indeed, they appear beyond credible answer.

A Grand Illusion

Nuclear disarmament advocates, church-based and secular, are correct that nuclear disarmament will require a transformation of the international system, to include a benign global orderer of some type to enforce disarmament rules judiciously and reliably. The problem is not these advocates' recognition of the need for global transformation to realize their nuclear disarmament goal; the problem is their failure to address seriously the feasibility of establishing and sustaining the new global order they recognize as necessary for nuclear disarmament, i.e., how to "get from here to there."[103]

As noted, disarmament advocates, religious and secular, point to a variety of dynamics, primarily including reason and "human genius," as the engines for this global

---

[103] Brad Roberts discusses this failure with regard to contemporary advocacy of the Treaty on the Prohibition of Nuclear Weapons. See, Roberts, "Nuclear Ethics and the Ban Treaty," op. cit.; and, Brad Roberts, "Ban the Bomb or Bomb the Ban? Next Steps on the Ban Treaty," *European Leadership Network, Global Security Policy Brief* (March 2018), available at https://www.europeanleadershipnetwork.org/wp-content/uploads/2018/03/180322-Brad-Roberts-Ban-Treaty.pdf.

transformation. Advancing the existing global order from the current "self-help," anarchic system of independent sovereign states to a new order governed by a benign and powerful "global body" or international institution(s) could indeed create a more peaceful system in which nuclear disarmament would be the prudent choice of some states and an imposed choice on others, as necessary.

The question, however, that once again must be asked is whether this is a plausible path to disarmament and an end to the threat of nuclear weapons. If not, time and attention would better be spent looking elsewhere; chasing after a grand illusion not only is a drain on energy and attention, it could easily lead to dangerous policy choices. U.S. national security policy might just as well be based on the expectation that the strident hostility that opponents exhibit by word and deed regarding the liberal world order the United States and allies seek to uphold will melt into cooperation and amity — a happy thought indeed, but unlikely to be a prudent basis for national security considerations.

This study focuses on the coherence and plausibility of recommendations frequently advanced in church-based and secular reports and studies, not on matters of theology. Nevertheless, it may be of interest to note here that the expectation that "the genius of man," "public opinion," or human progress will somehow drive the transition to an age of peace and disarmament, enforced by a benign "global body," does not comport with orthodox Christian theology. Aurelius Augustine of Hippo (St. Augustine), perhaps the greatest Christian theologian/scholar, was critical of war in the extreme, but taught that the age of amity and peace must await the second coming of the Messiah — when all is set right, including a new world order: "Whoever hopes for this so great good [i.e., a general peace] in this world, and in this earth, his wisdom is but folly."[104] Augustine's observation may or may not carry any weight with secular commentators, but it undoubtedly does and should within the broad Christian community—and is reflected in the German and French Catholic Bishops' 1983 pastoral letters.[105] Indeed, a fundamental presumption of the Just War Doctrine, to which Augustine contributed greatly, is that conflicting national interests leading to aggression are an ever-present possibility and that governments have the legitimate right and responsibility to protect the innocent from aggression.

The position expressed by Augustine and this corresponding fundamental presumption of the Just War Doctrine, minus the theological eschatology, is largely consistent with the Realist theory of international relations. This theory explains in *wholly secular* terms why—*absent* "some totally unanticipated happening," "a new cultural turn toward spirituality and universal humanism," a "black swan phenomenon," or widespread "personal and communal conversion"—the realization of a benign global body or institution(s) to enforce peace and disarmament is implausible.[106]

---

[104] Quoted in a classic analysis of St. Augustine's work. See Herbert Deane, *The Political and Social Ideas of St. Augustine* (Tacoma, WA: Angelico Press, 2013), p. 155.

[105] See, *Out of Justice, Peace: Joint Pastoral Letter of the West German Bishops, Winning the Peace: Joint Pastoral Letter of the French Bishops,* Edited by Schall, op. cit., pp. 67-68, 104.

[106] For a detailed discussion of Realist thinking see, Keith B. Payne, *Shadows on the Wall: Deterrence and Disarmament* (Fairfax, VA: National Institute Press, 2020), pp 17-36. "Christian realism," a school of thought most closely associated with renowned scholar Reinhold Niebuhr, largely parallels this traditional secular approach to international relations theory entitled Realism. See for example, Eric Patterson, "Eight Principles of Christian Realism," *Providence*, September 23, 2020, available at https://providencemag.com/2020/09/eight-principles-christian-realism-reinhold-niebuhr/.

Three Roadblocks

The roadblocks to disarmament via a cooperative transition
to an international system reliably governed by a benign
global orderer follow from *separate but related dynamics
occurring at different levels of analysis.*[107]   At least three
roadblocks exist whether the recommendation comes from
church-based or secular advocates. Is such a transition
impossible? Perhaps not. But if possible, it appears to be
without any foreseeable timeline given these three
seemingly insoluble problems — hardly a basis for prudent
national policy planning.

First, as noted above, at the individual level, if all
humans were cooperative pacifists, and reliably so, a new
world would be at hand and the road to disarmament easily
open. In 1788, James Madison observed in *The Federalist* No.
51, "If men were angels, no government would be
necessary. If angels were to govern men, neither external
nor internal controls on government would be necessary."
Madison's point, of course, is that humans are *not* angels
and *governing institutions are not led by angels*; they are led by
humans with all too-well-known foibles.

Institutions and individual humans obviously are
different in many ways — the following does *not* suggest
that individual humans and institutions are fully
analogous. But human institutions, consisting of and led by
humans, may reflect the frequently less admirable
characteristics of their leaders, including willful deception,
inconsistency, the lack of reliability and trustworthiness,
and aggressive ambition, *inter alia*. As James Stoessinger
concludes in his monumental historical survey of wars,
"With regard to the problem of the outbreak of war, the case
studies indicate the crucial importance of the personalities

---

[107] As in Waltz' classic three levels of analysis — the individual, the state
and the international system. See, Waltz, *Man, the State and War*,
passim.

of leaders. I am less impressed by the role of abstract forces, such as nationalism, militarism, or alliance systems.... In all these cases, a leader's personality was of critical importance and may, in fact, have spelled the difference between the outbreak of war and the maintenance of peace."[108] This reality of institutional behaviors reflecting the behavioral choices of their leaders contributes to the first seemingly insoluble problem.

In addition, institutional decision-making processes may introduce their own patterns of behavior that appear to parallel human imperfections, including a failure to abide by commitments, inattention to key developments, deceptive practices, the squandering of resources, biased favoritism, and a general lack of trustworthiness, *inter alia*. For example, in any global regime, the prospective changing of administrations and staffing (planned or not) or disagreements among them could create considerable inconsistency in the conduct of the global orderer— rendering it unreliable and untrustworthy in carrying out its commitments for constituents.

Absent a transition of all humanity to Madison's angels and/or the angelic, error-free functioning of the global regime, there is no reason to expect that the regime would actually function to meet expectations or that all prospective constituent members of the global body could be trusted to reliably disarm and cooperate in good faith. Those members with aggressive intent and untrustworthy character could retain military capabilities covertly or prepare covertly for a breakout of capabilities after others

---

[108] Stoessinger, *Why Nations Go to War*, op. cit., pp. 390-392. Another monumental survey of historical case studies also illustrates the role of individual leadership characteristics in decisions for war. See, Donald Kagan, *On the Origins of War* (New York: Doubleday, 1995), pp. 8, 569. See also, Bert Park, M.D., *Ailing, Aged, Addicted* (Lexington, KY: University Press of Kentucky), passim; and, Richard Ned Lebow, *Between Peace and War* (Baltimore: Johns Hopkins University Press, 1981), pp. 220-231.

had disarmed in whole or part. The latter nations would then be *highly vulnerable* to the former, particularly during the perhaps lengthy period of establishing the global orderer's power in strength. Prior to willingly giving up sovereignty and power to the global orderer, national leaders would have to consider that risk and find it acceptable. For those great powers with well-armed and untrustworthy foes, this could easily be too great a challenge—the risk of vulnerability despite the global regime could outweigh the expected benefit of subordination to a global orderer. Of course, if all nations were reliably cooperative and trustworthy, there would be no risk and this prospect would present no problem; but, if all nations were reliably cooperative and trustworthy, there would be no need for a transition of the international system to facilitate disarmament.

Adding further to this problem, prior to relinquishing sovereignty and power, national leaders would have to be confident that the global orderer itself, led by humans and potentially having its own sources of institutional error and misbehavior, would not *itself* have aggressive ambitions, a lack of attention to its advertised mandates and goals, deceptive practices, and engage in the unwarranted use of force. That is, in addition to the potential failure of the global regime to protect the constituent members reliably against the aggression of other members through error or connivance, the global orderer itself could become a threat to its constituents.

Why does this present a problem for a cooperative global transition and attendant disarmament? It is a problem because the question confronting national leaders when considering nuclear disarmament is not whether, in theory, a cooperative, reliable global authority would be a far superior alternative to the existing anarchic system; it is whether they could have sufficient confidence in the operation of a new global order and its orderer, on a

foreseeable timeline, to subordinate national sovereignty
and leave behind or hand over the arms they see as critical
for national security in the existing anarchic system. Such
confidence understandably is generally lacking now and, as
Colin Gray observed regarding leaderships that decline to
prioritize their nations' security, "That can, and upon rare
occasion has been tried, but we all should know that really
bad things tend to happen to states that decline to defend
themselves."[109]

Correspondingly, to give up national arms as would be
necessary for the establishment of the global orderer,
national leaders would need to have confidence that the
global authority would, in fact, ensure equal protection
under the law for all, while scrupulously refraining from
repression, oppression, or use of force other than to
discipline aggressors. This is a wonderful vision, of course,
but problematic because the global orderer envisioned
would itself be run and staffed by those who share human
imperfections and foibles—again, unless they are
Madison's "angels."

The prospect of a new global regime that is afflicted
with imperfections and errors, as inevitably would be the
case, is unlikely to inspire the needed confidence in national
leaders on a universal and near-simultaneous basis. They
could have little or no confidence that the new regime
would reliably provide the necessary protection while
refraining from repression, oppression, and the
unwarranted use of force—to the advantage of itself or
favored constituents, and to the disadvantage of others. The
experience of all history, including at the national level
where some particular affinities tend to help hold peoples
together, is that governments and human institutions of all
varieties, once established, have engaged in such behaviors

---

[109] Colin S. Gray, "Foreword," in, Keith B. Payne, *Shadows on the Wall:
Deterrence and Disarmament* (Fairfax, VA: National Institute Press, 2020),
p. xi.

to the extreme dissatisfaction of some constituents—as is demonstrated by the continuous lineage of political upheavals, rebellions, revolutions, and civil wars across the globe. Why, now, should we expect global governance not to reflect occasional or frequent errors of inconsistency, aggressive ambition and pugnacity? Why should it be expected that, somehow, a new global body of some variety would be error-free and transcend seemingly enduring human limits? Disarmament advocates offer no answer to this question, and typically avoid it altogether beyond vague speculation regarding "some totally unanticipated happening," "a new cultural turn toward spirituality and universal humanism," a "black swan phenomenon," or widespread "personal and communal conversion."

For example, a renowned proponent of a new global regime emphasized that the transition will require "a lot of courage, a lot of faith in the new order…"[110] The question, of course, is faith in what, and courage on the basis of what—the hope that, somehow, this new human institution would reliably, consistently operate as no other has in history? Many leaders responsible for national security could instead understandably see basing national policy on faith in the realization of such an institution not as courageous and faithful, but as imprudently placing their nations at potentially even greater risk than otherwise would be the case. There could be no assurances whatsoever that they would be wrong in that expectation.

Those leaderships with aggressive ambitions, *today* including contemporary Russia, China, North Korea, and Iran, are least likely to transfer power and sovereignty to a prospectively strong global authority that would then be charged with thwarting their aggressive designs and would have the power to do so. How could other national leaders with more benign intentions expect, with any confidence

---

[110] "Cronkite Champions World Government," op. cit., p. A2.

that, once in power, a new global orderer—subject to the same imperfections of seemingly all human institutions and interactions—would perform so reliably and judiciously as necessary, whether established in gradual steps or more rapidly? National governments—having ceded a measure of sovereignty and power to it—would be vulnerable to it and/or to other constituents ineffectively controlled by it. As Sir Michael Howard observed in the (above) quote, that prospect can hardly be attractive to national leaders with responsibility for national security.

Disarmament advocates may rightly be asked to identify a single human institution in all of history that has consistently behaved in the essentially error-free, faithful, cooperative, selfless manner necessary for the global orderer they envisage. In the United Nations itself, where employee loyalty is supposed to be to the global institution and its laudable stated goals, the divisive effects of parochial nationalism, competing national interests and ambitions, and other factors are evident in virtually every aspect of its activities.

Given these realities, establishing the universal and near-simultaneous consensus needed to establish a high-functioning global regime would seem unlikely in the extreme. Indeed, in those cases where national leaders appear to have demonstrated an unusual willingness to subordinate the quest for national power to some conception of the greater international good and amity, foes and potential foes typically have looked on their moves with unbridled suspicion—*not* an unreasonable response in an anarchic international system with frequently untrustworthy, inconsistent national leaderships.

This suspicion certainly was apparent most recently in the Russian and Chinese responses to the U.S. decade-long push for global nuclear disarmament and, similarly, in Russia's overwhelmingly skeptical response to Washington's repeated assurances that the United States would limit its missile defense capabilities in deference to notions of mutual deterrence "stability."[111]   Even had Russian and Chinese leaders fully accepted the sincerity of an individual administration's commitment to so limit the United States, they could have little confidence that subsequent U.S. governments would be similarly inclined. Again, these Russian and Chinese responses to the U.S. initiatives were reasonable given an anarchic international system and U.S. leaderships and governments that are subject to human foibles and imperfections, including inconsistency.

In short, the first seemingly insoluble problem is that— until all humans become Madison's angels and/or human institutions can be expected to operate near-flawlessly— human institutions, whether national, international or transnational, will reflect some seemingly enduring patterns of human behavior, for both good and ill. National leaders recognizing this reality understandably must be reluctant to abandon or hand over the critical means of national protection to a global regime that might then *not* provide adequate national protection reliably against misbehaving members and could itself become a grievous threat.   This latter prospect is the basis for Thomas Schelling's comment (above) that a powerful global orderer could itself become the despotic source of horrific violence, and thus the cause of rebellion and revolutions.   As Schelling says, "**some of us would have to turn around and start plotting civil war...**"[112]

Of course, if the seemingly enduring unscrupulous patterns of human and institutional behavior could be

---

[111] See for example, David Axe, "Why Does Russia Hate the THAAD Missile Defense System?," *The National Interest*, January 25, 2022, available at https://nationalinterest.org/blog/reboot/why-does-russia-hate-thaad-missile-defense-system-199715.

[112] Schelling, "The Role of Deterrence in Total Disarmament," op. cit., p. 405.

banished or reliably self-controlled, and cooperation and amity became the consistent norm—then the envisaged global body could indeed be possible.   In that case, however, as noted, a global institution to prevent war and enforce disarmament would hardly be needed. This new benign world would naturally be peaceful and national leaders could prudently "beat their swords into plowshares and their spears into pruning hooks."[113] Consequently and ironically, a global orderer able to mandate and enforce disarmament would likely become feasible when it is no longer needed for that purpose.

Until then, the probability seems very slight indeed that all great powers will, essentially simultaneously, take the potentially great risk of giving up sovereignty and their means of protection on the hope that other parties would reliably do the same, and that the world orderer thus created would escape history and human foibles, and benignly, reliably provide the protection they need when necessary. Nuclear disarmament advocates include little or no elaboration as to how and why the enigmatic dynamics they identify for the needed transformation should be expected to overcome these hurdles—hardly a reasonable basis for national security planning.

The *second* seemingly insoluble problem follows from the first. National leaders may well find some value in relatively weak international institutions, such as the past League of Nations and the contemporary United Nations. Indeed, the great powers have found some value in global institutions, but understandably have refused to provide them with the combination of power and authority that might seriously interfere with their own security requirements and ambitions.[114] That is, great powers may,

---

[113] From Isaiah 2:4.

[114] As an illustration of this point, the United Nations itself is designed to provide the permanent members of the Security Council with veto power over prospective U.N. actions. Consequently, when members of

for some purposes, welcome *weak* global institutions that do not pose a serious threat to their own sovereignty and power. The problem, of course, is that while relatively weak global institutions cannot pose a security threat to great powers, and thus may be acceptable, they also are incapable of reliably providing the needed order and universal protection under a global law — as has been demonstrated for over a century, first by the League of Nations and since by the United Nations.

In short, a *weak* global institution obviously is acceptable to national leaders, witness the United Nations, but is incapable of the needed global governance. A global institution so powerful as to control and reliably protect all powers, great and small, *could* in principle provide global governance, but is not acceptable to great powers for that very reason. The reluctance of national leaders to embrace a high-powered global institution is not unreasonable; it is a rational response to the fact that, as discussed above, absent the prevalence of Madison's angels, a powerful global orderer could *not* be relied upon to exercise its power for the adequate protection of all and to the disadvantage of none, and could itself become an existential threat. Some national leaderships could, in theory, accept the risks and decide to make the great leap to subordinate their national sovereignty and power in the hope for a grand outcome. But, as Professor Mearsheimer has observed, "It is unlikely

---

the Security Council disagree, the U.N. is effectively prevented from actions necessary to defend a member state — as has been illustrated yet again by the U.N.'s wholly toothless response to Russia's ongoing, naked aggression against Ukraine. This power arrangement within the U.N. is not an accident. As Richard Gowan, a senior U.N. official reportedly has observed, "It was Franklin Roosevelt who wanted to set up an organization that would police the world...But the only way he could get Russia and the other powers to agree to that deal, was if they had the ability to block any actions against themselves." Quoted in, Semier, "Why Isn't the UN Doing More to Stop What's Happening in Ukraine?" op. cit.

that all the great powers will simultaneously undergo an epiphany…";[115] and, "there is little reason to think that change is in the offing."[116]

A *third* problem confronting the disarmament advocates' agenda is that the two interrelated problems discussed above are not obviously subject to correction via the dynamics they generally identify, i.e., by reason, human genius, some new organizational structure, "rising powers in the non-West," "countries that embrace soft power," "action…grounded on a solid foundation of hope," or, "the normative force of the prohibition of acquiring nuclear weapons." These factors, powerful as they are or may become, are largely unrelated to the problems — the supposed powerful dynamics do not address the need.

How so? A lack of reason, inadequate genius, the fear of proliferation, etc., are *not* the causes of international mistrust and insecurity and the corresponding need for national arms to deter and defend. These fundamental problems appear unlikely to yield to human genius, reason, public opinion, some new analytical or communication tools or organizational structure because insecurity and arms ultimately are symptoms of a much deeper cause, i.e., the mistrust, suspicion and fears that flow from the combination of enduring, unfortunate, patterns of human behavior and state behavior, and the anarchic structure of the international system. It is not the lack of reason, information or concern about proliferation that compels national leaderships to seek and cling to national power for protection, including nuclear weapons; doing so can be a *fully reasonable and well-informed* choice because nuclear deterrence *can be valuable* given the combination of enduring patterns of human and state behavior, and the anarchic structure of the international system. This ongoing reality

---

[115] John Mearsheimer, "Realists as Idealists," *Security Studies*, Vol. 20, No. 3 (2011), p. 428.

[116] Mearsheimer, *The Tragedy of Great Power Politics*, op. cit., p. 362.

is not eliminated or concealed by soaring speculation about a new human consciousness, hope and courage, or by efforts intended to "educate" leaders otherwise, stigmatize nuclear weapons, and shame nuclear states.[117]

In short, the absence of reliable global cooperation and amity is not a matter of missing intellect or reason on the part of national leaders, but of seemingly enduring human and structural realities that bound the behavior of all countries that seek survival in an anarchic system. In spite of impressive advances in technology, medicine, farming, etc.,[118] there is little, if any, apparent evidence that the root causes of international insecurity and mistrust are abating. In truth, evidence of conflicting national interests, irreconcilable goals, insecurity, and the brutal use of force, and corresponding international mistrust and mutual suspicion, is manifest on a daily basis.

Disarmament advocates "educating" national leaders that nuclear weapons are dangerous and lack value cannot somehow create the needed international trust and amity. Those leaders well understand that nuclear weapons are highly lethal and dangerous. They also understand that past and immediate history readily demonstrates to anyone paying attention that nations can be unpredictable, untrustworthy, aggressive, and violent; their continuing mistrust, suspicion and fears often are fully justified in international relations. To be sure, nuclear deterrence is only a palliative in this context, but for many leaderships facing well-armed and dangerous foes, the hope for a global orderer and nuclear disarmament does not provide a

---

[117] As described in, Matthew Gault, "The Lawyer Working to Dismantle the World's Nuclear Weapons: Beatrice Fihn, executive director of the International Campaign to Abolish Nuclear Weapons, dreams of a world free from the threat of nuclear war," *Vice News* (Motherboard), December 16, 2020, available at https://www.vice.com/en/article/bvx7vv/the-lawyer-who-is-working-to-dismantle-the-worlds-nuclear-weapons.

[118] See Rothkopf, "The Case for Optimism," op. cit.

practicable alternative to deterrence on any workable timeframe.

In 2020, summarizing a lifetime of scholarly work on the subject, Professor Emeritus Colin Gray essentially repeated the prescient conclusion on the enduring need for prudent national defense efforts that he had made four decades earlier:

> To be blunt about it, the international political order just is what it is — an ultimately lawless "self-help" system. We cannot responsibly decline to pursue security because we do not like the available options. …Any rational person, one might think, should be able to design a very much more reasonable and safer global security system than we have today. I suspect that this is true but alas, entirely beside the historical point. Our current security and insecurity context is the unplanned, certainly unintended, product of centuries of political history… the best we can do is to make sensible use of our immense empirical experience. This will enable us to judge prudently what should, and what ought not be done as we strive, perhaps hopefully, to endure the darker possibilities of historical narrative.[119]

To risk repetition, this discussion should not be read as opposition to the ideal of a reliably cooperative world order. The existing anarchic system, dominated as it is by parochial ambitions, insecurity and corresponding competing quests for national power, works against the type of global cooperation that could help address global problems. However, it is unhelpful or worse for disarmament proponents to point to a new global orderer to mandate and enforce disarmament, when the dynamics

---

[119] Gray, "Foreword," in, Payne, *Shadows on the Wall: Deterrence and Disarmament*, op. cit., pp. xi-xii.

for transformation that they suggest will drive the creation of a global orderer are vague, obscure, arcane, transcendental, and unclearly related to the root problems. They typically focus on graphic descriptions of the effects of nuclear war and the need for change, perhaps rightly so, but are effectively silent on the fundamental question of how the roadblocks to the transition they advocate will be overcome and the realization of their vision so apparent that it can be the basis for prudent national policy planning.

Worse, in the absence of anything much useful to say about the operational feasibility or timeline for a global transition and nuclear disarmament, advocates' frequent disparagement of deterrence and efforts to "stigmatize" nuclear weapons threaten to undermine this tool *known* to provide limits on the prospect for nuclear aggression, at least on occasion (i.e., deterrence), in pursuit of a vision unlikely to be realized in any foreseeable timeframe for fully understandable reasons. A vision beset by seemingly insoluble problems and contradictions in getting "from here to there" is no real alternative and should not be considered the basis for rejecting the alternative known to provide a measure of limitation. Indeed, the ongoing campaign to so denounce nuclear weapons and deterrence is much more likely to have some restraining effect on Western democracies than on their authoritarian foes. This imbalance itself may contain the seeds of future international crises and catastrophe; this caveat seems not to bother at least some advocates.

Summary and Conclusion

In conclusion, secular and church-based advocacy of nuclear disarmament is strikingly similar. The assumptions and arguments of these two communities, knowingly or not, borrow heavily from each other. Secular advocates take as basic starting points the morality standards embedded in the Christian Just War Doctrine, i.e., the need to protect the innocent, minimize violence, oppose aggression, and avoid any use of force unrelated to protecting the innocent against aggression. Correspondingly, secular disarmament advocates and *some* church-based reports reach the common conclusions that those moral standards cannot accommodate the possession or employment of nuclear weapons, or nuclear deterrence.

Church-based analyses, curiously, often borrow heavily from the principles of a particular secular approach to deterrence, commonly known as a "balance of terror," in their opposition to the deployment of strategic *defensive* capabilities and more discriminate, lower-yield, nuclear weapons—which would seem to comport well with Just War guidelines. But they reject these capabilities, because, it is said, they are "destabilizing."

The common conclusion of these church-based and secular positions that follow from this intermingling of Just War morality standards and a particular deterrence theory is that the United States should both reject nuclear weapons and deterrence as too potentially risky and destructive, and also those types of capabilities that could hold out the potential for limiting that feared destruction in the event deterrence fails.

Church-based and secular disarmament advocates also often similarly conclude that deterrence, if acceptable at all, is only so on an interim basis—pending the creation of a global orderer capable of governing a cooperative disarmament process. Even their suggestions regarding the dynamics that supposedly can drive the transition to this new world order are similar and similarly amorphous. Their common conclusion is that energy and attention must be directed away from the maintenance of nuclear weapons and deterrence, and toward the pursuit of global transformation and disarmament as the alternative to nuclear deterrence.

The end of the Cold War brought widespread expectations that, somehow, international relations and human interactions had changed: Nuclear disarmament was widely expected, as was a cooperative new world order that would replace the constant episodes of great power warfare that had so characterized the past. But, a decade later, it once again is painfully obvious that the structural and behavioral conditions that underlie the reason countries seek and need armaments, including the benefits of nuclear deterrence, are much more resilient than the naïve *Zeitgeist* that followed the end of the Cold War.

It seems that this general lesson must be relearned with every new generation. In 1954, the great American diplomat, George Kennan, pointed to the same dynamic and idealist *Zeitgeist* in his assessment of the earlier, ill-fated 1925-1935 disarmament discussions under the League of Nations:

> It had been pointed out by thoughtful people, many years before these discussions began, that armaments were a symptom rather than a cause, primarily the reflection of international relations, and only secondarily the source of them. I know of no sound reason why, even in 1925, anyone should have supposed that there was any likelihood that general disarmament could be brought about by multilateral agreement among a group of European powers whose mutual political differences and suspicions had been by no means resolved. The realities underlying the maintenance of national armaments generally were at that time no more difficult to perceive than they are today.[120]

Nuclear disarmament may, someday, be possible. But the beginning of wisdom in this regard is to understand that

---

[120] George F. Kennan, *Realities of American Foreign Policy* (London: Oxford University Press, 1954), pp. 20-21.

a manifest transformation of the global order must precede disarmament, and that some powerful dynamic that is now, at best, nebulous, will have to drive that transition. The realization of that vision would almost certainly have to wait until that dynamic—whatever it may be—and resulting transition are so mature as to be fully apparent to leaders responsible for national security. The global orderer must be capable of the task of mandating and enforcing disarmament *without* also itself being a potentially despotic threat. The need for this transformation is a high bar and not a trivial detail; it is the single most fundamental point. Yet, the dynamics for this transformation identified by disarmament proponents are, at best, of dubious power and effect.

To misunderstand the challenges to the realization of disarmament is to misunderstand the basic realities of international relations—that the existing anarchic international system is highly resistant to the type of structural transformation recognized by virtually all as necessary for disarmament, i.e., a cooperatively-created global body able to mandate and enforce disarmament. This resistance is not because national leaders typically are foolish, uninformed or malevolent in this regard. It is because they are responsible for national security in an often unpredictable, dangerous, and anarchic international system.

The consequent problem for those advocating nuclear disarmament as their alternative to despised policies of deterrence is that their favored solution may superficially appear to be far safer and more attractive than is deterrence as a solution to the threat posed by nuclear weapons; it is a vision that inspires rousing exhortations and noble-sounding sentiment. In contrast, as noted British academic, Sir Lawrence Freedman, has rightly observed, nuclear deterrence, "was never likely to inspire a popular following. Campaigners might march behind banners demanding peace and disarmament...but successful deterrence, marked by nothing much happening, is unlikely to get the pulse racing. It has no natural political constituency."[121] That observation clearly is true, but a careful examination of the assumptions, evidence and logic of the proposed disarmament alternative to deterrence just as clearly demonstrates that it is unlikely to be practicable. This is *not* because leaderships reluctant to give up their national deterrents in favor of disarmament are ignorant, irrational or ignoble—and thus subject to remedial correction. It is because the anarchic structure of the international system and enduring patterns of human and state behavior combine to create roadblocks to transformation and security concerns that compel states toward the accumulation of power for national defense and survival.

Some leaderships may elect to advance policies geared toward disarmament but, until a new world order emerges, or an alternative, new form of deterrence is at hand, when disarmament aspirations are incompatible with sustaining nuclear deterrence, as they inevitably must be, for many the prudent priority option almost certainly will remain deterrence. This reality is reflected in the fact that, in a rare display of unity, all permanent members of the U.N. Security Council joined in rejecting the U.N.'s Treaty on the Prohibition of Nuclear Weapons (TPNW) and, as yet, not a single state reliant on nuclear deterrence for its security has signed it, including those that have otherwise been very active in the nuclear disarmament movement. The Biden Administration emphatically rejected it with the wholly realist observation that, "The United States does not share the underlying assumption of the TPNW that the elimination of nuclear weapons can be achieved irrespective of the prevailing international security environment. Nor do we consider the TPNW to be an

---

[121] Lawrence Freedman, *Deterrence* (Malden, MA: Polity Press, 2004), p. 25.

effective tool to resolve the underlying security conflicts that lead states to retain or seek nuclear weapons."[122]

Deterrence policies must, of course, be as safe, secure and non-provocative as possible, but disarmament as the alternative to nuclear deterrence appears implausible. Why so? Because, as Professor Kenneth Waltz concluded, "Nuclear weapons decisively change how some states provide for their own and possibly for others' security, but nuclear weapons have not altered the anarchic structure of the international political system."[123] In sharp contrast to prevalent church-based and secular calls for disarmament based on obscure dynamics and a wholly uncertain transformation of the international system, deterrence policies have a demonstrated measure of effectiveness for preventing war and its escalation in the existing anarchic environment. To be sure, deterrence is a palliative with inherent risks and the possibility of failure; a safer alternative to nuclear deterrence would be a great and unalloyed good.

However, cooperative global nuclear disarmament almost certainly is not a plausible alternative. For those leaders responsible for national survival and reliant on deterrence, moving to replace it with a vague and seemingly unattainable alternative, understandably and rightly, is unlikely to be judged a prudent policy choice. The resilience of this truth and its significance for recurring hopes for a new world order and disarmament seemingly must be relearned by every new generation. This need is illustrated by George Kennan's observation (quoted above) regarding the ill-fated disarmament conferences of the 1920s and 1930s and Sir Norman Angell's even earlier failed proposition about a "Great Illusion," as discussed in the

---

[122] Department of Defense, *2022 Nuclear Posture Review*, op. cit., p. 19.
[123] Kenneth N. Waltz, "Structural Realism after the Cold War," *International Security*, Vol. 25, No. 1 (Summer 2000), p. 5.

Preface.   Unfortunately, the elegance of disarmament advocacy and the beauty of the goal do not put it within reach.   President John Adam's well-known observation from 1770 fully applies: "I will enlarge no more on the evidence, but submit it to you...Facts are stubborn things; and whatever may be our wishes, our inclinations, or the dictates of our passions, they cannot alter the state of facts and evidence..."

About the Author

Keith Payne is a co-founder of the National Institute for Public Policy, a nonprofit research center located in Fairfax, Virginia and Professor Emeritus, Missouri State University, Graduate Department of Defense and Strategic Studies. In 2005, he was awarded the Vicennial Medal from Georgetown University for his many years on the faculty of the graduate National Security Studies Program.

Dr. Payne has served in the Department of Defense as the Deputy Assistant Secretary of Defense for Forces Policy and as a Senior Advisor to the Office of the Secretary of Defense (OSD). He received both the Distinguished Public Service Medal and the OSD Award for Outstanding Achievement

Dr. Payne also served as a Commissioner on the bipartisan Congressional Commission on the Strategic Posture of the United States and is a co-author of the Commission's final report (2009). He also served in Democratic and Republican administrations as a member of the Secretary of State's International Security Advisory Board, and as Chair of U.S. Strategic Command's Senior Advisory Group, Policy and Strategy Panel. He is an award-winning author, co-author, or editor of over 250 published articles and 40 books and monographs, some of which have been translated into German, Russian, Chinese, Japanese or Spanish. Dr. Payne's articles have appeared in major U.S., European and Japanese professional journals and newspapers. His most recent monograph is, *Tailored Deterrence: China and the Taiwan Question* (2022).

Dr. Payne received an A.B. (honors) in political science from the University of California at Berkeley in 1976, studied in Heidelberg, Germany and received a Ph.D. (with distinction) in international relations from the University of Southern California.

Index

governance, global, 67, 71
governments, 62
Gray, Colin, 20-1, 43, 66, 74
Great Illusion: A Study of the Relation of Military Power to National Advantage, The, 3

Howard, Sir Michael, 40-1, 68
human behaviors, 29, 37, 49, 61, 63
human genius, 57, 60-1, 72
humanism, universal. *See* universal humanism
Hussein, Saddam, 33

immorality, 12-15, 30-1, 35; *see also* morality
inconsistency, 67, 69
India, 34
insecurity, 27-8, 30
insecurity, international, 73
institutions, 63-4, 68
institutions, global, 51, 52, 62, 71
institutions, global (international), 61
institutions, international, 70
international accords, 29
international aggression, 37
international agreements, 42
international governance, 51
international institutions, 30, 36-7, 50
international law, 5
international relations, 10, 62, 73, 77-8
    dilemma, 27, 29
    past history, 40, 43
    security, 36-7
    world order, 46-7
international rules, 45
international systems, 40, 78-9
    proposed dynamics, 54, 60
    security, 30-2, 35-8
    world order, 46-7, 50, 52
Iran, 44, 67

Japan, 22-23, 24, 43
Just War doctrine, 14-21, 14n17, 41, 62, 76

Kennan, George, 77

law global, 71

suspicioun, 73

Taylor, Richard, 35n52
technologies, 39, 43
tensions, 45
territorial power, 3
threats, 28; *see also* survival, national
trade, 3
transformation, global, 60–1, 76
Treaty on the Prohibitions of Nuclear Weapons, 10, 49–50, 79
trust, international, 31, 53, 73
trust, mutual, 37, 40
trustworthiness, 64–5

Ukraine, 10, 21–2, 29, 34, 44, 46–7
United Nations, 9, 50, 52, 68, 71
United States, 24, 56, 68–9, 76
United States Conference of Catholic Bishops, 11–12
universal humanism, 55, 62, 67

warlike behaviors, 4, 5
weapons, biological and chemical, 27, 33, 39–40, 42
weapons of mass destruction, 28
Wilson, Woodrow, 58
Wittner, Lawrence, 50
world government, 48
world order, transformation of, 44–53
World Wars (I and II), 5, 52, 58

Commentary on
Chasing a Grand Illusion:
Replacing Deterrence With Disarmament

"Professor Keith Payne has tackled a knotty dichotomy that has put U.S. analysts of nuclear policy at loggerheads for decades — the call by moralists and idealists for nuclear disarmament, versus realists who see the imperative of maintaining nuclear deterrence. He delivers an exceptional analysis of why nuclear disarmament is not yet practical and the need for nuclear deterrence continues. Nuclear disarmament doesn't yield a condition of international peace and cooperation. It is the reverse. Only when these utopian ideals are reached — an improbable prospect given past and current history — is disarmament feasible. This conclusion is cogently and dispassionately explained in this exceptional essay."

Dr. Kathleen Bailey
former Assistant Director, Arms Control and Disarmament Agency,
and Deputy Assistant Secretary of State

"Keith Payne has done it again. In this treatise he lays out a concise but thorough examination of the arguments surrounding the potential risks and benefits of nuclear disarmament, the necessary geopolitical changes that would be required to move down a path to a 'world without nuclear weapons' and, most importantly, a clear-eyed assessment of the likelihood of achieving and sustaining those changes. This should be mandatory reading for those charged with formulating U.S. nuclear policy as well as in the halls of our military colleges."

General Kevin Chilton, USAF (ret.)
former Commander, U.S. Strategic Command

"Nuclear weapons and their elimination is too serious a subject just for advocacy and hope. In this penetrating study, Professor Keith Payne carefully examines arguments for disarmament — and finds them wanting. Payne does the topic the service of a sober, clear-eyed, and critical review. Anyone interested in this important topic would do well to consult this lucid report."

Elbridge Colby
former Deputy Assistant Secretary of Defense
for Strategy and Force Development

"Dr. Payne has written a definitive study of why nuclear weapons—not nuclear disarmament—provides sovereign states with security in an anarchic international system when no international institution can prevent others' aggression and enforce agreements and assure a cooperative order. Russia's invasion of Ukraine, despite the 1994 Budapest Memorandum that provided Ukraine with security assurances in return for nuclear disarmament, is a stark reminder that survival against more powerfully-armed aggressors, despite signed international accords, depends on a country's ability to deter—with arms that include nuclear weapons—or defeat an attacker. *Chasing a Grand Illusion: Replacing Deterrence With Disarmament* is a must-read for all Americans."

Amb. Joseph R. DeTrani
former Director, National Counterproliferation Center

"Since shortly after the dawn of the nuclear age critics of both a religious and secular bent have agitated for nuclear disarmament to spare mankind from the potential ravages of thermonuclear war. In this tightly argued essay, Keith Payne demonstrates why their prescriptions logically would require a radical transformation of the international order. However much we all might wish for it, that transformation is unlikely to happen and this powerful study in the spirit of the late Colin Gray and James Schlesinger reminds us why nuclear deterrence, with all its flaws, remains the most likely safeguard against a conflagration."

Amb. Eric Edelman
Counselor, Center for Strategic and Budgetary Assessments and
former Undersecretary of Defense for Policy

"Few would question the sincerity of the disarmament movement, but few are also willing to subject its most basic assumptions to careful scrutiny. Professor Keith Payne's paper highlights the poverty of the answers commonly given when disarmament activists face questions about how actually to achieve the radical transformation in global affairs, and perhaps in human nature, that their dream would require. This 'how to' question is of huge import, both morally and practically. The challenge of nuclear stability is quite real, after all, but as Payne points out, arguments for an impossible — or at least a wholly unpredictable and un-plannable — solution are essentially useless to the prudent policymaker. (Nor, moreover, can one be said to have a moral obligation to achieve the unachievable.) Payne does a commendable job of drawing attention to these problems which should be read by all those interested in this subject; one wonders how the disarmament community will answer his challenge."

The Hon. Christopher A. Ford
former Assistant Secretary of State

"To those who seek a world without nuclear weapons, Professor Keith Payne poses an unforgiving question: In a future, more benevolent world order, what are the necessary conditions under which all nuclear powers could safely disarm and, more importantly, what are the practical steps to achieve such a state? In his thoroughly-researched and thoughtfully-argued piece, Dr. Payne concludes that given today's anarchic international system, and still dangerous world, there is no prospect for achieving nuclear disarmament in the near term. Moreover, in light of man's foibles, and the shortcomings of international institutions created by man, such a transformation is, much as he might wish it weren't so, simply implausible even in the long term. Dr. Payne's work provides the intellectual framework that is, without doubt, central to any future debate on these matters."

Dr. John R. Harvey
former Principal Deputy Assistant Secretary of Defense
for Nuclear, Chemical, and Biological Defense Programs

"This book is an invaluable reality check in a field where people are often tempted by simple solutions and idealist aspirations that, if implemented, could yield disastrous outcomes, however well-intentioned. Professor Keith Payne masterfully interrogates assumptions and the logic of arguments to guide us to the conclusion that credible deterrence is a worthy aim. It's an indispensable text at a dangerous time."

Rebeccah Heinrichs
Senior Fellow, Hudson Institute

"To quote T.E. Lawrence: 'All men dream, but not equally.' This is most evident in the debate over the value, and the very morality, of nuclear weapons. In this monograph, Professor Payne is scrupulously objective in presenting the positions of disarmament advocates, both religious and secular, who would banish nuclear weapons for the sake of peace and humanity. But as the reader encounters each successive argument in favor of disarmament, it becomes ever more apparent that aspirations cannot substitute for sound policy in a dangerous world. By exposing the fallacies of the nuclear disarmament movement, Dr. Payne makes an important contribution to our understanding of why and how nuclear weapons and nuclear deterrence remain essential components of our national security."

Amb. Robert Joseph
former Under Secretary of State for
Arms Control and International Security

"This study is an invaluable contribution to our understanding of nuclear deterrence and disarmament. Most proponents of effective nuclear deterrence dismiss disarmament advocacy in just a few sentences. Dr. Payne may be the first to analyze in considerable, appropriate detail the reasons for, and impracticality of, disarmament ambitions. In doing so, he strengthens the case for continued effective deterrence."

Dr. Susan Koch
former Senior Advisor, Department of State

"In *Chasing a Grand Illusion*, Professor Keith Payne — one of the world's leading scholar-practitioners on the subject of nuclear weapons — dismantles arguments in favor of nuclear disarmament by systematically showing that the elimination of nuclear weapons globally remains implausible absent a fundamental transformation of the international system. He persuasively argues that, for the foreseeable future, nuclear deterrence will remain the only available means for the United States to protect itself from growing nuclear dangers. This book is a must-read for anyone interested in nuclear weapons policy, but especially for those who may be tempted by the false allure of near-term nuclear abolition."

Professor Matthew Kroenig
Government and Foreign Service, Georgetown University

"In a balanced evaluation of the arguments for and against the policy of nuclear deterrence, Professor Keith Payne provides a clear picture of current international affairs, the self-interest that drives diplomacy and the acquisition and stockpiling of nuclear weapons. His short volume is a reality check given the unstable state of affairs created by Russia's invasion of Ukraine and an adversarial posture between the U.S. and China."

Professor Victor Matthews
Missouri State University

"With his customary incisiveness and precision, Dr. Keith Payne cuts through what so many regard as the Gordian knot of the inability to reconcile those who accept, even if reluctantly, the deterrence value of nuclear weapons and those who do not, by identifying the root cause of which their acceptance or non-acceptance is merely a symptom. In short order, he clears away the brush, accumulated over the past half-century, that has obscured the fundamental arguments essential for understanding why things are the way they are in a world informed by nuclear weapons."

Dr. John Mark Mattox
National Defense University

"Cogently constructed and brilliantly delivered, Professor Keith Payne laconically examines the contemporary and decades-old arguments for replacing nuclear deterrence with global disarmament. He skillfully explains why the requisite transformation of international conditions needed before disarmament can occur is implausible. As the book's title suggests, expecting such a transformation is the 'grand illusion.' A must read for nuclear deterrence believers and deniers alike."

Colonel Curtis McGiffin, USAF (ret.)
Vice President and Co-Founder,
National Institute of Deterrence Studies

"Professor Keith Payne has written a masterful deconstruction and demolition of the vain hope that nuclear disarmament will bring about a peaceful and more stable world. In a clear and compelling fashion, backed by significant research into realms both secular and spiritual, he demonstrates that nuclear weapons have in fact prevented the outbreak of major conventional war between the Great Powers, thereby saving countless lives. The carnage, both human and material, which Russia is today inflicting upon Ukraine stands as a stark reminder of what NATO Europe might look like if stripped of its nuclear shield. Dr. Payne's work should be required reading for every strategist or policy maker."

The Hon. Franklin C. Miller
Principal, The Scowcroft Group

"Professor Keith Payne returns with trenchant analysis to a debate that started during the Manhattan Project, whether the United States should pursue general nuclear disarmament. His answer—that disarmament is neither feasible nor desirable absent dramatic and currently hard-to-foresee changes in the global security environment—represents a bipartisan consensus on U.S. nuclear policy that has existed for decades. This consensus must be sustained and reinforced in order to ensure that the United States retains a safe, secure and effective nuclear deterrent for the indefinite future."

The Hon. Jim Miller
former Under Secretary of Defense for Policy

"Professor Keith Payne's latest book, *Chasing a Grand Illusion*, addresses questions of deterrence and disarmament. To take on these questions, no one has a comparable background in practical, academic, theoretical, and real-world experience. His conclusion is that a transition to the cooperative world order needed to realize disarmament is implausible, and, therefore, deterrence remains a necessity. Anyone doubting that conclusion need only witness the destruction Russia is now inflicting on the people of Ukraine. The key issue leading to his conclusion is the enduring and reasonable lack of trust—in adversaries, global institutions and even alliances—inherent in the anarchic international system. Is it plausible that a new cooperative and trustworthy world order is emerging to enable disarmament? Dr. Payne explains as never before why it is a 'grand illusion' to believe so. This work should be required reading for all policy makers and keen students of the subject."

Dr. John P. Rose
Department Head, Defense and Strategic Studies Program
Missouri State University

"In [t]his persuasively argued monograph, Professor Keith Payne carefully examines the arguments of nuclear disarmament advocates. He demonstrates convincingly that these arguments, whether church-based or secular, suffer not only from serious logical inconsistencies, but are often built on unrealistic expectations about a radical transformation of the international system. Hence, they cannot serve as prudent guidance for U.S. security policy, which must continue to rely on nuclear deterrence."

Michael Rühle
Head, Climate and Energy Security
NATO International Staff

"Keith Payne's latest book is an extraordinary read. A realist, sober and timely reminder that well-meant peaceful intentions and wishful thinking in the area of nuclear disarmament do not necessarily lead to desired outcomes. In fact, the opposite is true — if implemented, it would weaken deterrence. A must read in times of intensified Russian nuclear saber-rattling."

Dr. Petr Suchý
Department of International Relations
and European Studies, Faculty of Social Studies
Masaryk University, Brno, Czech Republic

"In *Chasing a Grand Illusion: Replacing Deterrence With Disarmament,* Professor Keith Payne meticulously and comprehensively explains the faulty reasoning behind arguments that nuclear deterrence is dangerous and immoral and must be replaced by the elimination of nuclear weapons. He marshals facts, logic, and history to highlight the impracticality of nuclear abolition in an increasingly volatile and dangerous world and the implausibility of the solutions proffered by disarmament advocates. His book is an expert tutorial on the illusory appeal of the disarmament agenda and the reasons why a nuclear-free world does not equate to a safer one."

The Hon. David J. Trachtenberg
former Deputy Under Secretary of Defense for Policy

"In this tightly packed piece, Professor Keith Payne provides a comprehensive and balanced treatment of the most fundamental issues in the argument for disarmament vs. deterrence. These comments are largely restatements regarding two of those issues. Advocates for disarmament agree with the skeptics that a new global order will be required to make the risk of disarmament less than the risk of deterrence. This would give a global institution power over national sovereignty which would require the consent of each nation. The consent would have to be irrevocable, and the power would have to include both capability and process for enforcement. I know of no precedent for such power and processes.

Further, one of the most fundamental charges for the U.S. government is found in the Preamble to the Constitution, 'to provide for the common defense.' So long as government and governed see nuclear weapons as essential to the defense, there is no prospect for willingness to accept the risk to the common defense in surrendering such control to a global institution. As to the moral argument against deterrence, it is likely that the founding fathers placed high moral value on protecting the nation's citizens with the common defense.

We have more than 75 years of experience with some level of nuclear deterrence. We have years of experience with negotiated reductions in strategic nuclear weapons and some types of non-strategic weapons. We have no experience in eliminating the nuclear deterrent. Absent any such experience, the breadth and depth of the unknowns are likely to deter any responsible government from accepting the risk."

General Larry D. Welch, USAF (ret.)
former Commander, Strategic Air Command and
Chief of Staff, United States Air Force

www.ingramcontent.com/pod-product-compliance
Lightning Source LLC
Chambersburg PA
CBHW051504270326
41933CB00021BA/3457